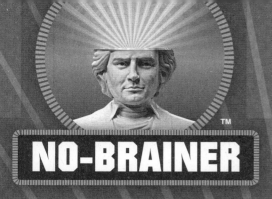

NO-BRAINER ™

MW00389987

WE MAKE PLAYING PIANO A NO-BRAINER!

Alfred
SINCE 1922

Alfred Music Publishing Co., Inc. • P.O. Box 10003 • Van Nuys, CA 91410-0003

alfred.com

Copyright © MMIX by Alfred Music Publishing Co., Inc.
All rights reserved. Printed in USA.

ISBN-10: 0-7390-6252-2 (Book & DVD)
ISBN-13: 978-0-7390-6252-4 (Book & DVD)

Beethoven bust photo courtesy of www.Statues.com

 Printed on 100% recycled paper.

2

CONTENTS

About the Authors 5

How to Use This Book and DVD 6

Part 1: The Basics 7

Sitting at Your Instrument 7
Sitting at the Piano
Sitting at the Electronic Keyboard

Hand and Finger Position 8
Fingering

The Keyboard and Pitch 9

Finger Warm-ups on the Black Keys ... 10

**The Musical Alphabet and the
Names of the White Keys** 11

Finger Warm-ups on the White Keys .. 12

Rhythm 13
Merrily We Roll Along
Go Tell Aunt Rhody
Aura Lee

Time Signatures 16
Right in Time
Four Beats Left to Go
Time for Both
Au Claire de la Lune

The Treble Staff 18
Old Woman on the Right
Mary Had a Little Lamb

The Bass Staff 20
Old Woman on the Left
Frère Jacques

The Grand Staff 22

The Whole Rest 23
Ode to Joy
Frère Jacques—Right and Left
Ode to Joy (with Two Hands)
Merrily We Roll Along

The Half Rest 25
Lightly Row

The Quarter Rest 26
Quarter March
A Restful Day
A Stitch in Time
Anna's March

Dynamic Markings 28
Loud and Soft
Three Ways to Play

Melodic 2nds 30
Who's on Second?

Melodic 3rds 31
Third Dimension

Harmonic 2nds and 3rds 32
Sweet and Sour

Melodic 4ths 33
Go Fourth and Make Music!

Melodic 5ths 34
Fifth Avenue

Harmonic 4ths and 5ths 35
Jingle Bells

Middle C Position 36
Middle C Rock

The Flat Sign 38
B Flat, B Blue
Walk in the Park
Rockin' All Night Long

G Position 40

Harmonic 3rds, 4ths and 5ths 41
G Rock

Tied Notes 42
Tie Exercise

Dotted Half Notes 43
Auld Lang Syne

3/4 Time Signature 44
Anna's Waltz

The Natural Sign 45
Tied and True Blues

The C Major Chord 46
Largo (Theme from the
New World Symphony)

The Pickup 47
When the Saints Go Marching In

The G7 Chord 48
Mary Ann

The F Major Chord 50
For He's a Jolly Good Fellow

Eighth Notes & Eighth Rests 52
Simple Gifts

The Sharp Sign 54
  Für Elise

The Dotted Quarter Note 55
  Eine Kleine Nachtmusik

More Dynamic Markings 57
  Blue and True
  Theme from a Mozart Sonata

Melodic & Harmonic 6ths 59
  Sixth Sense

Melodic & Harmonic 7ths 60
  Seventh Heaven

Octaves 61
  Octaboogie

Half Steps & Whole Steps 62

The Key of C Major 63
  C Major Scale Split

Practicing the C Major Scale 64

Tempo Markings 65
  C Major Scale Exercise

Articulation 66
  Slide, Bounce, and Bang

Ritardandos & Fermatas 67
  Good Morning to You

²⁄₄ Time Signature 68
  Russian Folk Dance

Primary Chords 69
  Triads
  Primary Progression

Chord Inversions 70
  Primary Chords in the Key of C Major
  Solid State

The Sustain Pedal (Damper Pedal) 71
  Bach Prelude in C

The Key of G Major 73
  G Major Scale
  Primary Chords in the Key of G Major

The Key Signature 74
  All Through the Night
  Minuet in G

A Piece in Two Keys 76
  Burleske

Alouette 77

Tempo & Expression 78

Triplets 79
  Beautiful Dreamer

⁶⁄₈ Time Signature 80
  Alphabeats
  The Irish Washerwoman

The Key of F Major 82
  F Major Scale
  Primary Chords in the Key of F Major
  Joy to the World

A Piece in Three Keys 84
  Three-Key Rock

Repeats 85

Minor Keys 86
  Scherzo

Harmonic Minor 88
  Primary Chords in Minor Keys

Symphony No. 40 90

Waves of the Danube 92

The Entertainer 94

Part 2: Rock 96
  The Workhorse of Rock: The Triad 96
    Babylon

  Minor Chords 99

  House of The Rising Sun 100

  Major And Dominant 7th Chords 101
    First Call

  Minor 7th Chords 103
    Isle of Dreams

  An Introduction to Rock Rhythms 104
    Syncopation
    Rhythm Exercises
    Rhythmic Independence
    Over the Top
    Under the Depths

  Basic Bass Lines 108

  Get 'Em Up 109

  Arpeggios and Chord Inversions 110

  House of the Rising Sun: Arpeggios . . . 111

  Chord Inversions 112

  Slash Chords 113
    Back to Babylon
    Better Voice Leading Through Inversions
    7th Chord Inversions
    Down to Earth
    Pedal Tones

4

Blue Fire 117

Reading a Lead Sheet 118
  Three Types of Lead Sheets
  Song Form Terminology
  Three Charts
  Riding On the Wind: Melody Lead Sheet
  Riding On the Wind: Rhythmic Notation Lead
  Sheet
  House of the Rising Sun:
    Chord and Slash Lead Sheet

More Left-Hand Patterns 122
  Boogie-Woogie Patterns
  Walkin' & Talkin'
  This Rock'n'Roll Thing
  Octaves
  Miles From Nowhere
  Almost There
  Broken Octaves
  All Night Station
  Boogie Lines in Octaves
  Saloon Spider

Beginning Improvisation 130
  Pentatonic Scales
  Deeper River
  Far As You Like
  The Minor Pentatonic Scale
  New Life
  Off the Main Highway

The Blues 139
  The Blues Scale and Blue Notes
  See the Light
  The Grace Note
  The Blues Shuffle or Swing Eighths

Roadhouse Deluxe 142

Honky Tonk Town 144

No Easy Riders 146

The 12-Bar Blues 147

Transposing 147

Take to the Road 148

Blues Line in the Bass = Rock
  Power Riffs 150

Funky Sixteenths 152
  Explosive Soul

Part 3: Being a Professional
Keyboardist 154
  Choosing Your Equipment 154
    Keyboards
    Samplers
    Modules
    Amplification
    Stands and Setups
    Your First Rig

  Using Your Keyboard's Sounds 158
    Keyboard Instrument Sounds
    Harpsichords, Clavinets ("Clavs") and Mellotrons
    Other Instrument Sounds
    Using Pads
    Synthesized Sounds

  Creating a MIDI Setup 167
    Basic Gear
    Using Different Kinds of Pedals and Effects
    Setting up Your MIDI Studio

  Getting Into a Band 173
    How to Get Into a Band
    Auditions

  Rehearsing and Gigging with a Band . . . 176
    Rehearsal Tips
    Making a Demo Recording
    The Gig: Before, During and After

  Understanding the Music Business . . . 180
    Gigs and Contracts
    The Recording Industry
    The Record Deal
    Promotion and Distribution
    Lawyers
    The Shape of Things to Come

  Getting a Manager 184
    What to Expect from a Manager

Part 4: Reference 186

  Chord Reference 186

  Major Scales 204

  Minor Scales 209

  The Circle of Fifths 224

About the DVD

The DVD contains valuable demonstrations of all the instructional material in Part 1. You will get the best results by following along with your book as you watch these video segments. Musical examples that are not performed with video are included as audio tracks on the DVD for listening and playing along. The audio tracks are all accesible through the chapter selection on your DVD player and also as downloadable mp3 files on your computer.

ABOUT THE AUTHORS

The Meeting of Great Minds
In order to enlighten you, we have gathered together a stellar group of authors who specialize in different facets of teaching piano. Every one of them has contributed knowledge to make playing piano a no-brainer. Here is a little information on each of them.

Joe Bouchard
Joe is one of the founding members, and bassist, of the legendary rock band Blue Öyster Cult. He has recorded the bass parts on every album from the band and sometimes played the keyboard parts as well—especially on the songs he wrote. Today, Joe continues to perform and teach guitar, bass, and piano. He is the author of many instructional books and videos published by the National Guitar Workshop and Alfred Music Publishing.

Jon Dryden
Jon began learning piano at the young age of five, and while in high school he had the honor of studying with jazz piano great Dr. Billy Taylor. After graduating from the Berklee College of Music, Jon found success playing in the New York City music scene. He has performed with Pat Metheny, Gary Burton, Phil Collins, Michael Brecker, and Victor Bailey and is currently an in-demand sideman and studio musician in New York. Jon provides invaluable information on playing in a band and the music business.

Nathaniel Gunod
Nathaniel is co-owner and managing editor of National Guitar Workshop Publications, co-owner of DayJams, and associate director of the National Guitar Workshop, which specializes in guitar, bass and keyboard instruction. His work as an editor and producer has included collaborations with such artists as George Benson, John Abercrombie, Joe Satriani, and many others. Nat is the author of many best-selling instructional books for piano, guitar, and music theory.

Amy Rosser
Amy Rosser has been a dedicated piano educator since the early 1980s, having taught at Goucher College in Maryland and Dickenson College in Pennsylvania. She has also led music history seminars in London and has successfully prepared many serious young musicians for music school auditions. Amy is a seasoned performer who has played throughout Europe and the U.S., performing with some of the world's most celebrated musicians. She is a member of Baltimore's Pro Musica Rara, a group devoted to the performance of early classical music on period instruments.

Kate Westin
Kate's love of music goes back to her early childhood where she was a pianist and vocalist. After years of performing and private instruction, she studied music composition and piano at the University of Southern California where she graduated with honors. Kate has dedicated many years to teaching piano privately and has edited numerous instructional books. Her skills as an editor brought her to Alfred Music Publishing where she is now a successful editor.

6

HOW TO USE THIS BOOK AND DVD

No Brainer™: Play Piano provides all the information you need to get started playing any keyboard instrument. The DVD contains video explanations of the basic techniques and musical concepts, as well as audio demonstrations of the pieces and exercises to help you reach your maximum potential on the keyboard.

Like most students, you may find it best to have your DVD player positioned near your instrument so that you can use the book as you watch and play along with the video. Sometimes you might prefer to work first with the book before using the video, carefully reading the instructions and playing the music. Other times, you may want to start by watching the demonstration. You decide what works best for you. There is no wrong way to use this book and DVD!

If you have an acoustic piano, whether it is a spinet, upright, or grand piano, you have all of the advantages of wonderful *touch sensitivity*. This means that you will be in complete control of the type of piano sound you make.

If you are just getting started and do not own a piano, it is a good idea to buy an electronic keyboard that is completely portable. Many keyboards will even operate with batteries and have their own internal speakers. Perhaps the most interesting feature of an electronic keyboard is the opportunity to choose different sounds for each piece of music. You will find suggestions in this method for different sounds to use. When shopping for an electronic keyboard, it is a good idea to choose one that has touch-sensitive keys so that you can vary the loudness and softness of the music with the force of your touch.

Here are some important things anyone learning to play music should keep in mind:

- **It is better to practice a little a lot than to practice a lot a little.** In other words, never miss a day of practice, even if you spend just a few minutes. Skipping a few days of practice and then practicing once for a long time will not be nearly as helpful as regular practice.

- **The quickest way to play fast fluently is to take the slowest route.** You will learn to play fast music by practicing slowly. Playing too fast too soon can lead to confusion, difficulty and bad habits that will slow your progress. The tortoise wins the race!

- **Practice with a metronome.** A metronome is an adjustable device that beats time for you. Electronic metronomes are inexpensive and very accurate. Get one that makes a click loud enough for you to hear. Practicing with a metronome will teach you to play with correct rhythm.

Although this book is perfect for a self-directed student, **there is no substitute for a good teacher.** A teacher can watch and listen to you play, and give you guidance and encouragement to do your best.

PART 1: THE BASICS

SITTING AT YOUR INSTRUMENT

Sitting at the Piano

- The bench must face the keyboard squarely.

- Sit on the edge of the bench exactly in front of the middle of the keyboard.

- Lean slightly forward.

- Relax and let your arms hang loosely from the shoulders.

- Adjust the distance of the bench from the keyboard so that when your hands are on the keyboard, your arms are parallel to the floor.

- Your knees should be slightly under the keyboard.

- Your feet should be flat on the floor. One foot may be slightly forward.

Sitting at the Electronic Keyboard

This is exactly the same as sitting at the piano, but be careful with the height of the stand or table on which the keyboard is sitting. Adjust the keyboard stand or the table/chair combination you are using so that your arms are perpendicular to and level with the keyboard.

VIDEO EXAMPLE

HAND AND FINGER POSITION

- Curve your fingers. From above, you should see a row of knuckles but no fingernails.

- Curve the thumb slightly inward. No hitchhiker thumbs!

- There should be a hollow spot big enough for a ping-pong ball to fit in your palm.

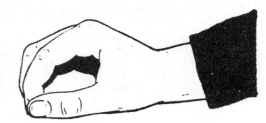

- Fingers are used like levers with the motion coming from the joint that attaches the finger to the hand.

- Push the keys down with the tips of the fingers.

- Keep your fingernails very short!

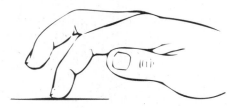

Fingering

Fingering numbers, which appear as the numbers 1 through 5, show which fingers to use to play. They can be found above or below the music. Each number corresponds to the same finger on either hand, with both thumbs being number 1 and both pinkies being number 5.

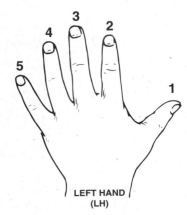

LEFT HAND
(LH)

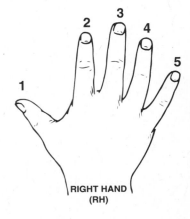

RIGHT HAND
(RH)

VIDEO EXAMPLE

THE KEYBOARD AND PITCH

The *keyboard* is made up of white and black *keys*. These keys are laid out in a repeating pattern, with black keys in groups of two and three. Each group of black keys is separated by two white keys.

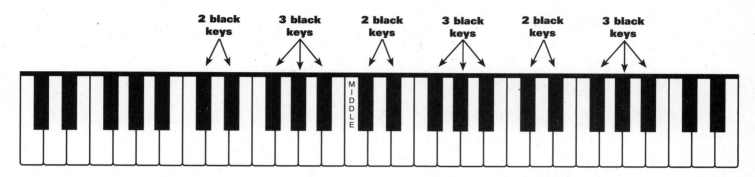

Pitch is the highness or lowness of a sound. On the piano keyboard, the pitch goes down to the left, and goes up to the right. As you move to the left, the pitches sound lower. As you move to the right, the pitches sound higher.

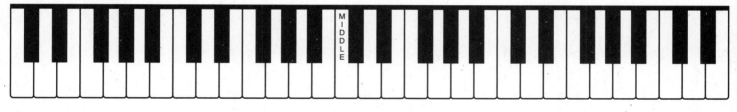

LOW SOUNDS ⬅ **DOWN (Lower)** **UP (Higher)** ➡ **HIGH SOUNDS**

DID YOU KNOW?

Award-winning pianist and singer/songwriter Norah Jones brought new attention to jazz keyboard sounds with her 2002 album *Come Away With Me*. Her unique blend of pop and jazz has made her one of the world's most popular performers.

Photo: © Tim Mosenfelder/Corbis

FINGER WARM-UPS ON THE BLACK KEYS

To get your fingers moving on the keyboard, play these exercises on the black keys.
The illustrations show which fingers to use on which black keys.

The numbers represent the fingers you will use to play.
Read from left to right and play at a slow, even pace.

Black-Key Warm-up for the Right Hand

RH

1	2	3	2	1	1	1
1	2	3	2	3	4	4
5	4	3	2	1	1	1
1	2	3	4	5	1	1

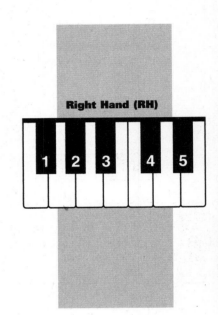

Right Hand (RH)

Black-Key Warm-up for the Left Hand

LH

5	4	3	4	5	5	5
5	4	3	4	3	2	2
1	2	3	4	5	5	5
5	4	3	2	1	5	5

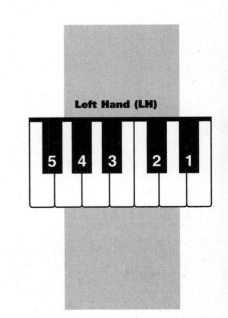

Left Hand (LH)

VIDEO EXAMPLE

THE MUSICAL ALPHABET AND THE NAMES OF THE WHITE KEYS

There are seven letters in the *musical alphabet:*

A B C D E F G

They repeat over and over:

A B C D E F G A B C D E F G A B C   and so on.

Every key on the piano has a name from the musical alphabet. The illustration below shows the names of the white keys. Notice that the C nearest the middle of the keyboard is called *middle C.* This is an important marker to memorize.

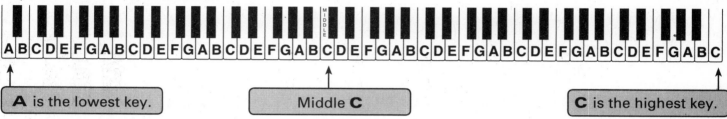

A is the lowest key.   Middle C   C is the highest key.

TIPS

If you are using an electronic keyboard with fewer than 88 keys, middle C is still the C closest to the middle of the keyboard. The highest and lowest notes, however, may be different than those shown above.

Notice that every C is always directly to the left of a group of two black keys.

Every F is directly to the left of a group of three black keys.

Find all of the C's and all of the F's on your keyboard.

FINGER WARM-UPS ON THE WHITE KEYS

Now let's try playing on the white keys. In these warm-ups, the notes are black circles with the name of the key to be played inside. The finger numbers appear **above** notes played with the right hand (**RH**) and **below** notes played with the left hand (**LH**).

Finger: 1

Note: **C**

One of the reasons that music notation is easy to read is that it looks the way it sounds. As the pitch goes up, the notes look higher on the page; as the pitch goes down, the notes look lower on the page. The warm-ups below are great examples of this.

Right-Hand Warm-up No. 1

Start on middle C. This is the right-hand C Position.

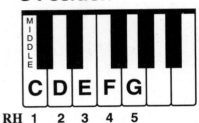

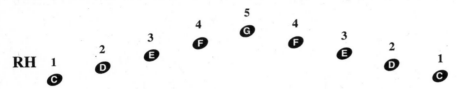

Right-Hand Warm-up No. 2

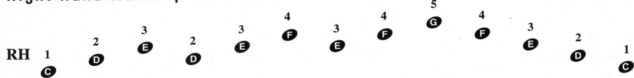

Left-Hand Warm-up No. 1

Start on the C below middle C. This is the left-hand C Position.

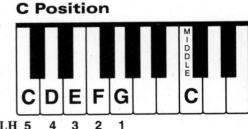

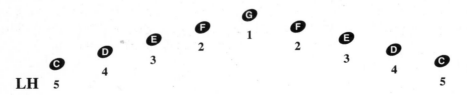

Left-Hand Warm-up No. 2

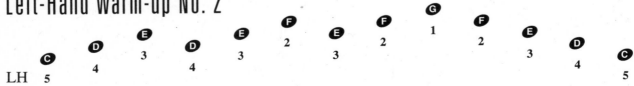

RHYTHM

Rhythm is the arrangement of long and short sounds into patterns. We measure the lengths of these sounds by counting *beats*. A beat is a unit of musical time; it is the pulse that keeps the music alive. When you tap your foot as you listen to music, you are tapping the beats.

We write rhythms with notes.

Play four quarter notes on middle C with your right hand. Count four steady beats aloud ("1, 2, 3, 4"), giving each quarter note one beat.

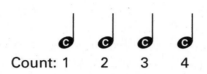

Count: 1 2 3 4

Play two half notes on middle C with your right hand.
Count four steady beats aloud, giving each half note two beats.

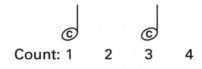

Count: 1 2 3 4

Play a whole note on middle C with your right hand.
Count four steady beats aloud.

Count: 1 2 3 4

Using the music below as a guide, first play four quarter notes on middle C with your right hand, one note for each count. Then, play two half notes, playing one note for every two counts. Then play a whole note, counting to four while you hold the note. Each group of four counts, or beats, is called a *measure*. Music is divided into measures with *bar lines*, and a *double bar* is used at the end.

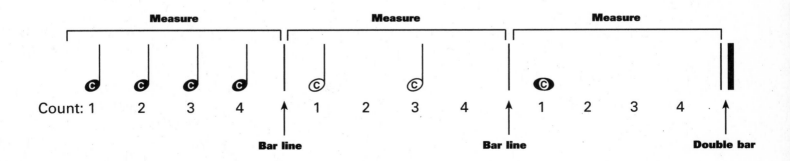

Enjoy playing these melodies. At first, count aloud as you play.

After you learn to play these, experiment with your electronic keyboard and try playing them with some interesting sounds.

AUDIO EXAMPLE

Merrily We Roll Along

Traditional

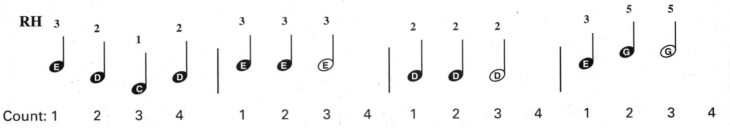

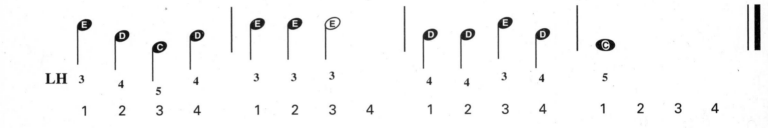

DID YOU KNOW?

Billy Joel discovered classical piano music at the age of four, and his love for the style that provided such a great technical foundation for his playing has never ended. With a smart urban sensibility and tremendous talent for composing music in a variety of styles, he is considered to be one of the most influential singer/songwriters of our time.

Photo: © Ken Settle

Go Tell Aunt Rhody

Traditional

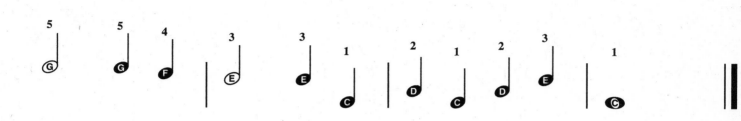

Aura Lee

Traditional

TIME SIGNATURES

At the beginning of every piece of music are numbers called the *time signature*. The time signature tells us how to count the music.

4
The top number tells how many beats are in each measure.
A **4** means there are **four** beats in each measure.

4
The bottom number tells what kind of note gets one beat.
A **4** means a **quarter note** ♩ gets one beat.

Right in Time

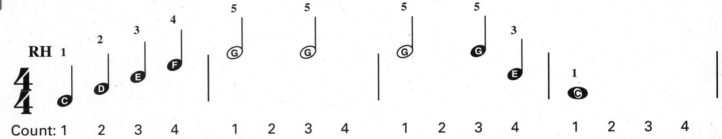

Four Beats Left to Go

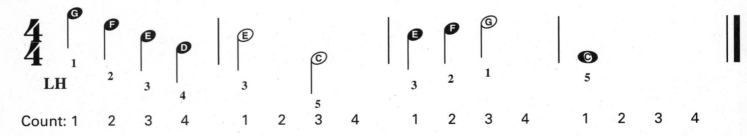

Count carefully and keep a steady beat.

Try a flute sound for these pretty tunes!

Time for Both

Au Clair de la Lune

French Folk Song

Count: Ê1 2 3 4   1 2 3 4   (etc.)

VIDEO EXAMPLE

THE TREBLE STAFF

In music notation, specific notes are indicated by their placement on a *staff*, which is made of five horizontal lines and the four spaces in between.

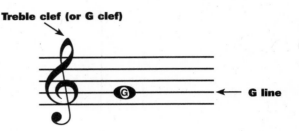

Music for the right hand is written on the *treble staff*, which is marked with a *treble clef*. The treble clef is sometimes called the *G clef* because the line it encircles is called G. A note placed on that line will be a G note.

As the music moves up through the musical alphabet, each note is written on the next-higher space or line. As the music moves down—backward through the alphabet—each note is written on the next-lower space or line. Notice that D is written on the space just below the staff, and middle C is written on a short line below the staff called a *leger line.*

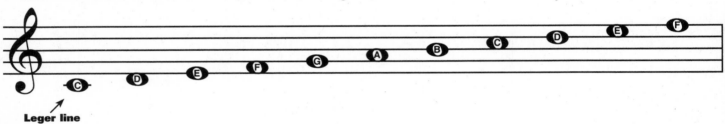

The spaces of the treble staff are easy to remember because, from bottom to top, they spell the word **FACE**.

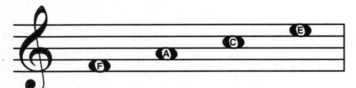

You can remember the notes on the lines of the treble staff using the sentence **Every Good Boy Does Fine**.

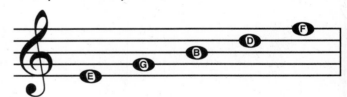

Here is the right-hand C position and the notes on the treble staff.

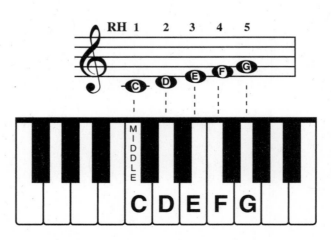

Here are some C-position pieces on the treble staff for you to play. As you can see, the music still looks the way it sounds: As the pitch ascends, the notes look higher on the page; as the pitch descends, the notes look lower on the page. Longer notes take more space, shorter notes take less space.

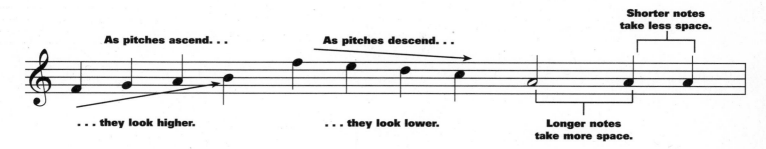

Old Woman on the Right

Traditional

Mary Had a Little Lamb

Traditional

THE BASS STAFF

Music for the left hand is written on the *bass staff,* which is marked with a *bass clef.* The bass clef is sometimes called the *F clef* because the line surrounded by the dots is called F. A note placed on that line will be an F note.

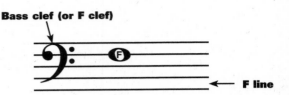

Just like the notes on the treble staff, as the music moves up through the musical alphabet, each note is written on the next-higher space or line. As the music moves down, each note is written on the next-lower space or line.

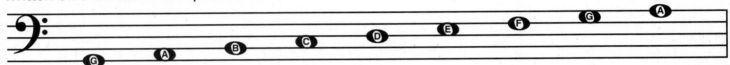

You can remember the notes on the spaces of the bass staff using the sentence **All C**ows **E**at **G**rass.

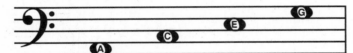

You can remember the notes on the lines of the bass staff using the sentence **G**reat **B**ig **D**ogs **F**ight **A**nimals.

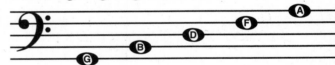

Here is the left-hand C position and the notes on the bass staff.

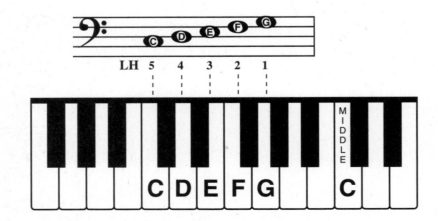

Here are some C-position pieces on the bass staff for you to play.

Old Woman on the Left

Traditional

Frère Jacques

French Folk Song

DID YOU KNOW?

During a time when the guitar dominated the world of music, Elton John redefined the role of the piano in rock. With a flamboyant style of performing, he became one of the most influential keyboard artists of the 1970s and 1980s. In addition to a phenomenal recording career, he has achieved great success as a composer for hit Broadway musicals such as *Aida* and the *Lion King*.

Photo: © Ken Settle

VIDEO EXAMPLE

THE GRAND STAFF

Piano music is written on a *grand staff,* which has a treble staff
and a bass staff that are connected by barlines and a *brace*.

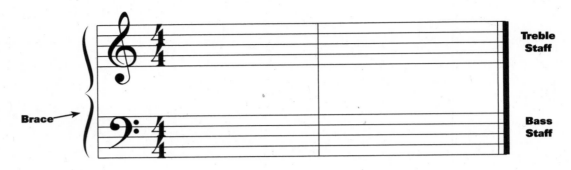

Here is C position and the notes on the grand staff.

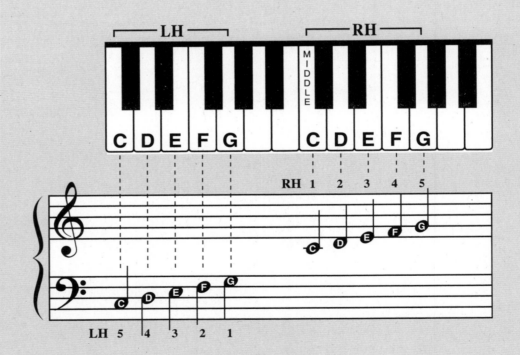

THE WHOLE REST

A *whole rest* indicates an entire measure of silence.

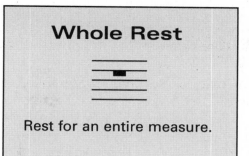

The following pieces will give you some practice reading music on the grand staff. Notice that while one hand is playing, the other is resting.

Try a big orchestral sound for this melody from Beethoven's Ninth Symphony.

Ode to Joy

Ludwig van Beethoven

Frère Jacques—Right and Left

French Folk Song

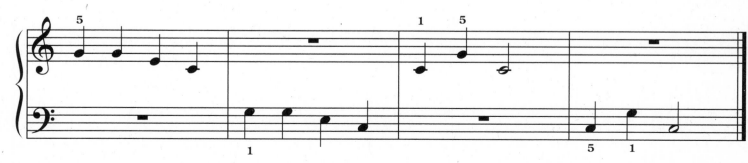

Below is another version of "Ode to Joy." This time, you'll play with both hands together. Keep your hands in C position and keep your eyes on the music. Learning to play by "feel" will make you a better sight-reader.

It is helpful to learn each hand individually before playing with both together.

TIPS

AUDIO EXAMPLE

Ode to Joy (with Two Hands)

Ludwig van Beethoven

AUDIO EXAMPLE

Merrily We Roll Along

Traditional

THE HALF REST

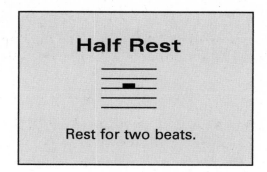

A *half rest* indicates two beats of silence.

Be careful not to confuse the half rest with the whole rest. Notice that the half rest sits on top of the third line while the whole rest hangs below the fourth line.

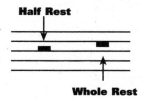

This exercise will prepare you for "Lightly Row," which combines half rests in one hand with notes in the other.

Lightly Row

Traditional

THE QUARTER REST

A *quarter rest* indicates one beat of silence.
It looks a little bit like a bird flying sideways.

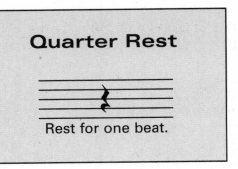

Quarter Rest

Rest for one beat.

The following pieces will let you concentrate on counting
rests because they use only one hand at a time.

Quarter March

Count: 1   2   3   4   1   2   3   4   (etc.)

A Restful Day

Count: 1   2   3   4   1   2   3   4   1   2   3   4   1   2   3   4

(etc.)

Let's put the hands back together. First, learn each hand individually, counting carefully. Remember to keep your eyes on the music.

A Stitch in Time

Anna's March

DYNAMIC MARKINGS

One of the ways we make music more enjoyable and interesting is by varying the volume at which we play. Musicians refer to these changes in volume as *dynamics*, and *dynamic markings* are used in written music to indicate the various degrees of loud and soft.

To the right are two important dynamic markings. Each one is an abbreviation of an Italian word that describes the volume. (Italian is the international language of music.)

$\boldsymbol{f}$ *forte* (loud)

$\boldsymbol{p}$ *piano* (soft)

On a keyboard with weighted keys (such as an acoustic piano and some electronic keyboards), play loud by using more weight in the arm and wrist as you drop into the key; use less weight to play soft. On a keyboard that does not have weighted keys, use a more forceful finger motion to play loud, and use a more gentle finger motion to play soft.

Electronic Keyboards: If you are playing an electronic keyboard with touch-sensitive keys, you will be able to affect dynamics with your fingers as described above. If your keyboard does not have touch-sensitive keys, you may have to change the sound selection or use the volume control to create changes in dynamics.

Play all the loud notes equally loud and all the soft notes equally soft.
Keep a steady beat, and be careful not to play faster when you play louder or slower when you play softer. Have fun with this study in contrasts.

Loud and Soft

Here is another important dynamic marking:

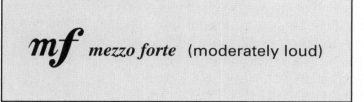

Concentrate on making a clear difference between the different dynamics in this piece.

Three Ways to Play

Photo: © Ken Settle

Tori Amos began playing piano at the young age of two and a half. With her original, technically fluid keyboard stylings and remarkable talent for elegant, inventive songwriting, she began attracting what is now a huge loyal following with the release of her 1992 album *Little Earthquakes*.

MELODIC 2NDS

An *interval* is the distance between two notes. On the keyboard, the interval from one white key to another adjacent white key, up or down, is called a *2nd*. When two notes are played one after the other, as notes are played in a melody, the interval is called a *melodic interval*.

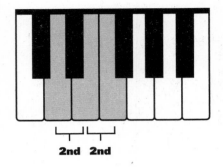

Notice that 2nds are written from a **line to a space**, or a **space to a line**.

Some of the melodic 2nds in the following piece are labeled for you; see if you can label the rest.

Who's on Second?

MELODIC 3RDS

To play a 3rd, skip a white key.

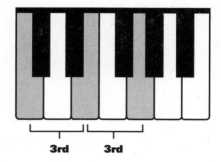

Notice that 3rds are written from a **line to a line**, or a **space to a space**.

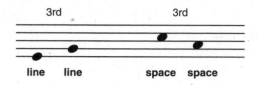

Some of the melodic 3rds in the next piece are labeled. Try labeling the rest yourself.

Third Dimension

HARMONIC 2NDS AND 3RDS

When we play two notes together, we create *harmony*, and the intervals between these notes are called *harmonic intervals*. The 2nds and 3rds you have learned as melodic intervals can also be played as harmonic intervals.

Play these harmonic 2nds and 3rds, and notice that the 2nds have a *dissonant* (clashing) sound and the 3rds have a *consonant* (harmonious, sweet) sound.

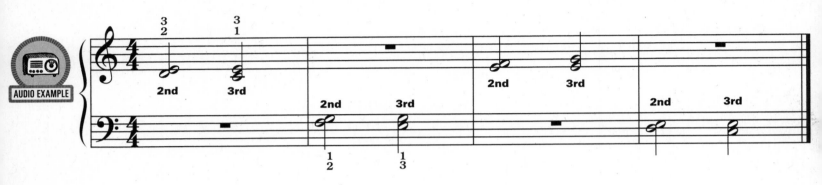

Now that you're playing notes together with a single hand, it is even more important to learn each hand separately before putting them together.

Sweet and Sour

MELODIC 4THS

To play a 4th, skip two white keys.

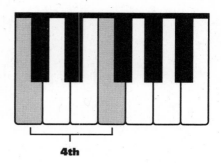

4th

Notice that 4ths are written from **line to space** or **space to line**, like 2nds. You will find that this is true for all even-numbered intervals.

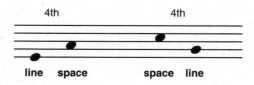

Some of the 4ths in this piece are labeled; you label the rest.

Go Fourth and Make Music!

34

MELODIC 5THS
VIDEO EXAMPLE

To play a 5th, skip three white keys.

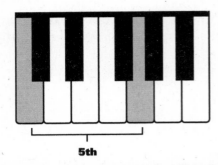

5th

Notice that 5ths are written **line to line** or **space to space**, like 3rds. You will find that this is true for all odd-numbered intervals.

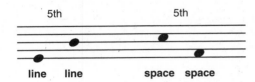

5th   5th

line   line   space   space

GIVE IT A TRY

One 5th is labeled in the following piece; you label the rest.

Fifth Avenue

AUDIO EXAMPLE

DID YOU KNOW?

After more than four decades, jazz and fusion great Chick Corea continues to enjoy a career that reflects the evolution of contemporary keyboard playing. With such diverse influences as Mozart, Charlie Parker, Beethoven and Bud Powell, his innovations include exciting experimentation with electronic music.

Photo: Courtesy of Chick Corea Productions

HARMONIC 4THS AND 5THS

This exercise has some harmonic 4ths and 5ths, and some harmonic 2nds and 3rds appear in the third and fourth measures. At the end of the exercise is a repeat sign, which means to go back to the beginning and play the exercise again.

Enjoy playing this popular winter song that uses harmonic intervals in the left hand.

A bell sound would be perfect!

GIVE IT A TRY

Jingle Bells

James Pierpoint

VIDEO EXAMPLE

MIDDLE C POSITION

In middle C position, the first finger of each hand is used to play middle C.
Two new bass clef notes are played by the left hand: A and B.

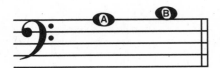

TIPS

Here are the important things to remember about middle C position:

- Both thumbs are on middle C.
- The right hand is positioned exactly the same as in C position learned on page 18.
- The left hand has fifth finger on F.

Here is middle C position and the notes on the grand staff.

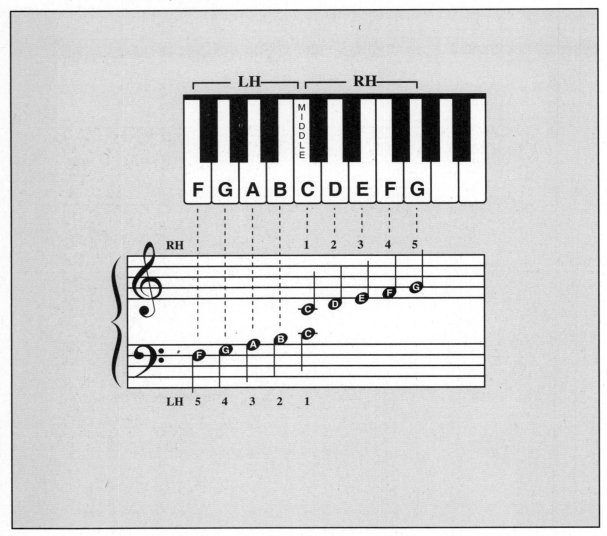

Here's a tune that's played in middle C position. Say the names of the notes aloud as you play until the bass clef A and B notes are fully learned.

Middle C Rock

Photo: Robert Knight

? DID YOU KNOW?

Whether blues, rock, country, or gospel, Ray Charles mastered them all. His versatility and command of the keyboard made this legendary singer, songwriter and composer one of the most popular entertainers of all time.

THE FLAT SIGN

A *flat sign* ♭ before a note means to play the next key to the left, whether it is a black key or a white key.

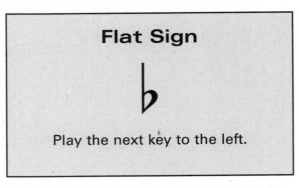

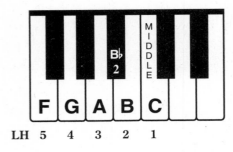

A flat sign is one of several symbols that are called *accidentals*. When an accidental appears before a note, it applies to that note for the rest of the measure. If the accidental does not appear again in the next measure, the note in question returns to its natural position.

This tune is played in middle C position and includes some flat notes.

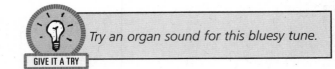

B Flat, B Blue

These pieces will give you some more practice reading flats in middle C position.

Walk in the Park

Rockin' All Night Long

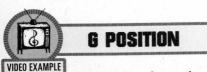

G POSITION

G position introduces several new notes: low B, low A, and low G in bass clef for the left hand and A, B, high C, and high D in treble clef for the right hand.

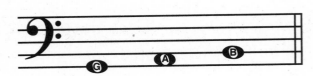
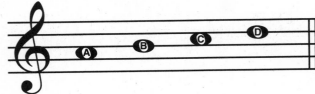

Here is G position and the notes on the grand staff.

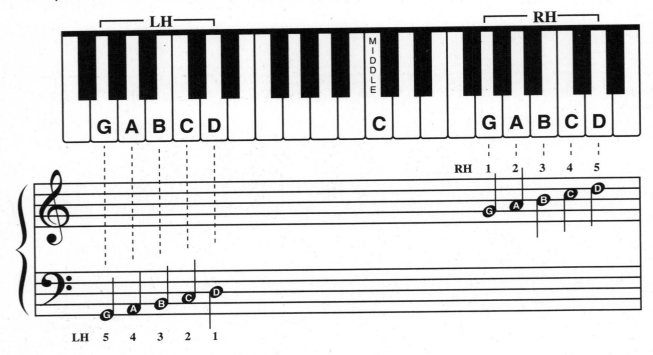

Practice playing the notes in G position, reciting the names of the notes aloud as you play.

HARMONIC 3RDS, 4THS AND 5THS

This exercise will prepare your left hand to play the next piece. It uses harmonic 3rds, 4ths and 5ths.

 AUDIO EXAMPLE

Be sure to learn each hand alone before playing hands together. Practice slowly at first.

TIPS

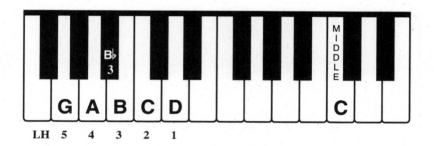

 AUDIO EXAMPLE

G Rock

This piece has a definite rock 'n' roll feel, so try one of your keyboard's cool synth sounds. It will also sound great with an electric piano sound.

GIVE IT A TRY

TIED NOTES

A *tie* is a curved line that connects two notes of the same pitch. Two notes connected by a tie are *tied notes*. The second tied note is not struck; rather, the key is held down for the combined values of both notes.

This is a great way to write notes that are longer than one measure...

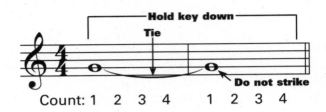

...or to start a long note on the fourth beat of a measure.

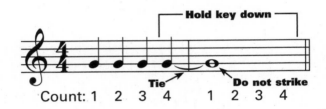

In this C-position exercise, the right hand has notes tied over the bar line into measures 2, 4 and 6. Meanwhile, the left hand plays on the first beat of every measure. Count aloud as you play.

Tie Exercise

DOTTED HALF NOTES

Adding a dot to the right of a note increases its value by half. Since a half note gets two beats, a dotted half note gets three. A dotted half note is equal to a half note tied to a quarter note.

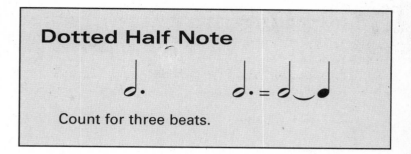

Dotted Half Note

Count for three beats.

Next New Year's Eve, you can entertain your fellow revelers with this classic tune, which is almost all in C position. In measure 7, reach with your second finger to play E and your hand will be perfectly positioned for your fifth finger to play the A in measure 8 without having to reach. Also, notice that the melody starts in the left hand and moves to the right, then returns to the left hand at the end.

Choose a great holiday sound that will be heard over the merriment, such as brass or string orchestra.

Auld Lang Syne

Traditional Scottish Melody

VIDEO EXAMPLE

¾ TIME SIGNATURE

Often called *waltz time*, ¾ time has three beats per measure.

A **3** means there are **three** beats in each measure.

A **4** means a **quarter note** ♩ gets one beat.

AUDIO EXAMPLE

Anna's Waltz

DID YOU KNOW?

Sarah McLachlan studied classical guitar, piano and voice before signing her first recording contract at the age of 17, and has since become a three-time Grammy Award winner. In 1997, she founded the Lilith Fair, a music tour that focused on female singer/songwriters.

Photo: © Ken Settle

THE NATURAL SIGN

Notice that a *natural sign* is used in the next tune to indicate a B-natural after a B-flat within the same measure. A natural sign returns a note that has been changed by an accidental to its unaltered position.

This bluesy tune uses ties to shift the emphasis off of the strong beats (beats 1 and 3) and onto the weak beats (beats 2 and 4). This is called *syncopation*.

Tied and True Blues

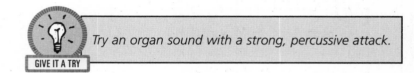

Try an organ sound with a strong, percussive attack.

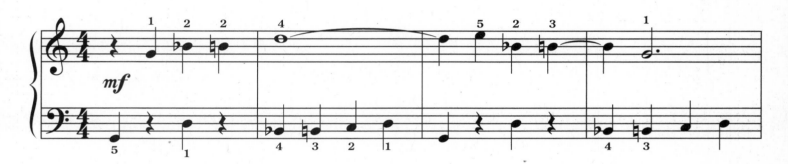

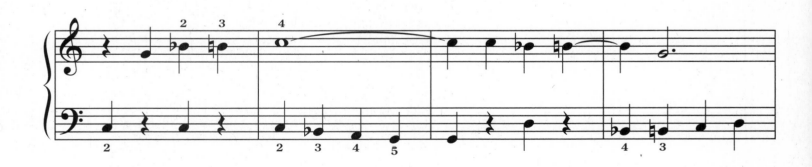

VIDEO EXAMPLE

THE C MAJOR CHORD

A *chord* is a combination of three or more notes played together. The *root* of a chord is the note that gives the chord its name. The note C is the root of the *C major chord*, which is made up of the notes C–E–G.

It is very important to play all three notes exactly together, keeping your fingers curved. Practice these C major chords with your left hand.

AUDIO EXAMPLE

C Major Chord Warm-up (Left Hand)

AUDIO EXAMPLE

Largo
(Theme from the New World Symphony)

GIVE IT A TRY

Since this melody is from one of the most famous classical symphonies, try it with an orchestral string sound.

Antonin Dvořák

THE PICKUP

When one or more notes are played before the first full measure at the beginning of a piece, it is called a *pickup*. The pickup measure is an *incomplete measure*. Frequently, when a piece begins with a pickup, the last measure will also be incomplete so that the rhythmic values of the two combined equal one full measure.

Practice the C major chord with the right hand before playing "When the Saints Go Marching In."

C Major Chord Warm-up (Right Hand)

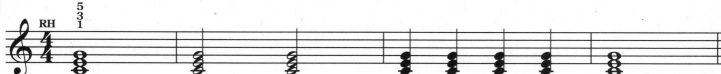

When the Saints Go Marching In

"When the Saints Go Marching In" is an American spiritual commonly played by New Orleans Dixieland jazz bands. It will sound great played with a brass sound.

American Spiritual

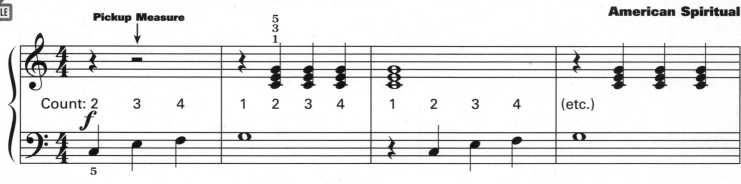

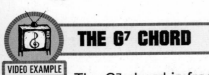

THE G⁷ CHORD

The G⁷ chord is frequently used with the C major chord. Notice that, unlike the C major chord, the root of this chord is not played as the lowest note. This is called an *inversion*.

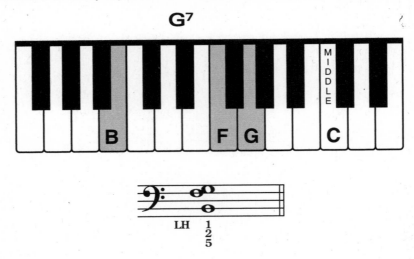

These exercises will help you learn to switch between playing the C and G⁷ chords.

No. 1

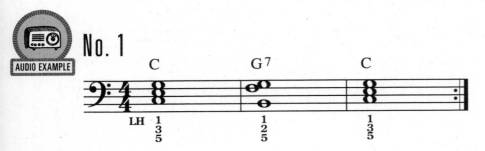

No. 2

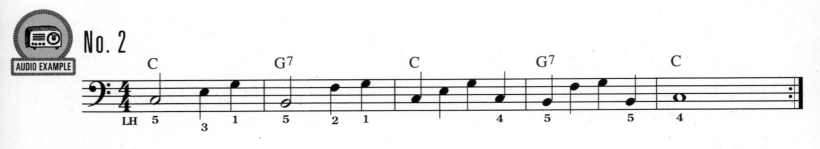

No. 3

This piece has the melody in the right hand and combines harmonic
2nds and 3rds with chords in the left-hand accompaniment.

Mary Ann

Traditional

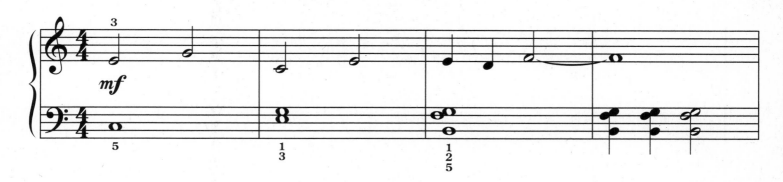

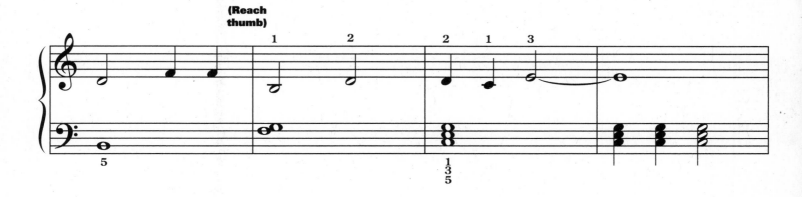

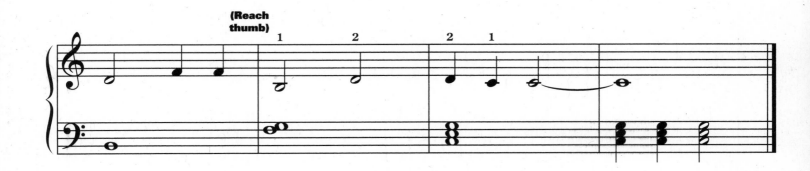

THE F MAJOR CHORD

The *F major chord* often appears with the C major and G⁷ chords. Like the G⁷ chord you learned on page 48, the F major chord you will play is an inversion.

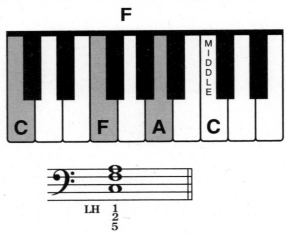

Practicing these exercises will help you learn to play the F major chord in combination with C major and G⁷.

No. 1

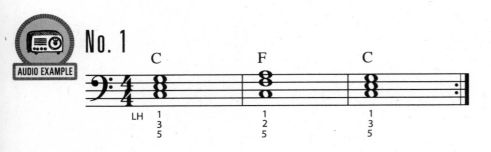

No. 2

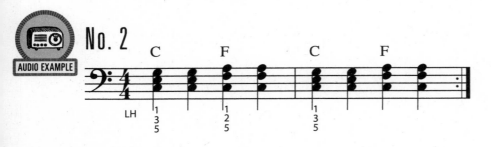

No. 3

For He's a Jolly Good Fellow

Traditional English Folk Song

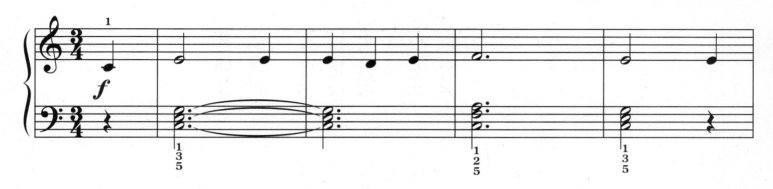

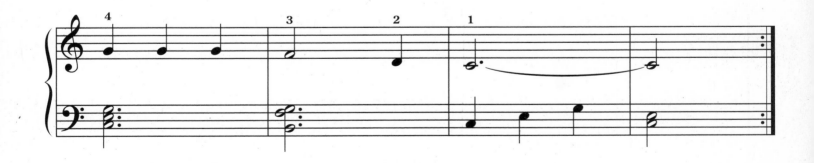

EIGHTH NOTES & EIGHTH RESTS

The duration of an eighth note or eighth rest is one-half beat, which is half as long as a quarter note. Music with eighth notes is counted by dividing the beat into two halves.

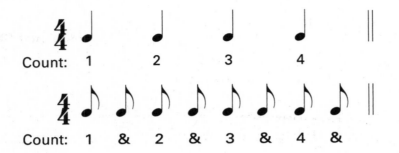

Groups of eighth notes are often connected with beams and grouped into beats. Compare the notes below to the single eighth notes above.

If an eighth note occurs on only one subdivision of a beat, it will usually appear as a single note with a flag. An eighth rest will take the other half of the beat if there is no note.

The following diagram shows the relative values of the types of notes and rests you know so far.

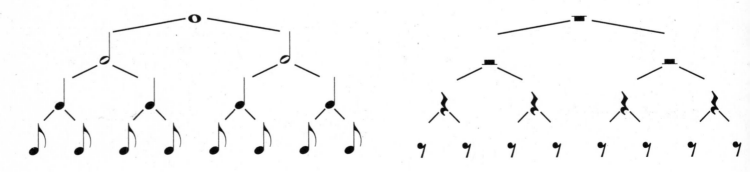

Simple Gifts

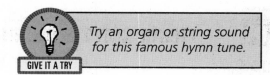
Try an organ or string sound for this famous hymn tune.

This piece uses eighth notes in both hands.

Traditional Shaker hymn

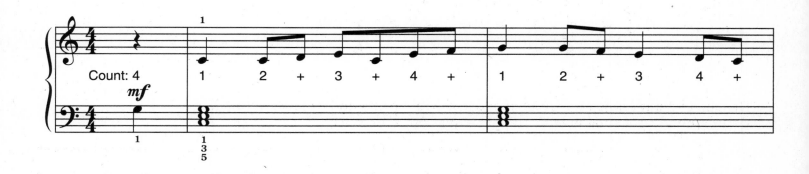

THE SHARP SIGN

A sharp sign ♯ before a note means to play the next key to the right, whether it is a black key or a white key. It is an accidental that means the opposite direction of a flat.

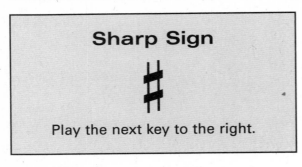

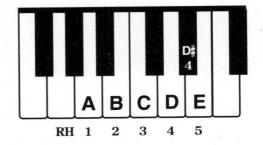

All the rules that apply to flats also apply to sharps: when a sharp appears before a note, it applies to that note for the rest of the measure unless cancelled by a natural sign.

Für Elise

Ludwig van Beethoven

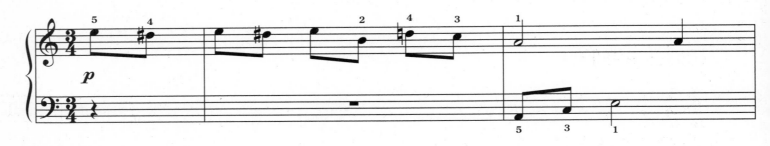

VIDEO EXAMPLE

THE DOTTED QUARTER NOTE

A quarter note tied to an eighth note is held for one and a half beats. An eighth note or eighth rest works nicely to take up the other half of the beat:

An easier way to show this rhythm is with a *dotted quarter note*. Since a dot increases a note by another half of the note's value, the dotted quarter note is equal to one and a half beats.

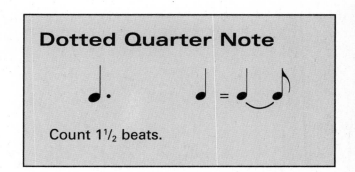

Here are some familiar tunes that use the dotted quarter note rhythm.

London Bridge

Alouette

Silent Night

Eine Kleine Nachtmusik

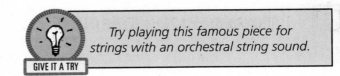

Try playing this famous piece for strings with an orchestral string sound.

Wolfgang Amadeus Mozart

Same note, different finger!

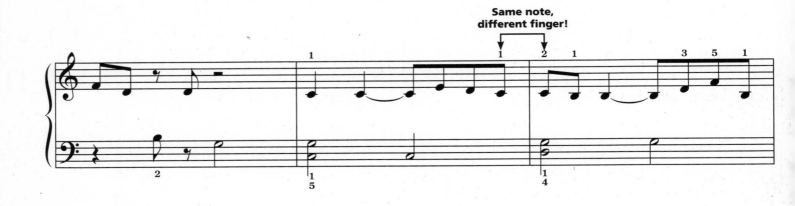

MORE DYNAMIC MARKINGS

Here are some new important dynamic markings:

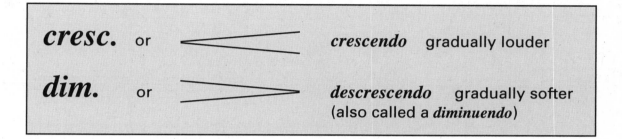

mp	*mezzo piano*	moderately soft

cresc. or ‹	*crescendo*	gradually louder
dim. or ›	*descrescendo*	gradually softer (also called a *diminuendo*)

Blue and True

Be sure to play crescendos and decrescendos as gradual, not sudden, changes in loudness.

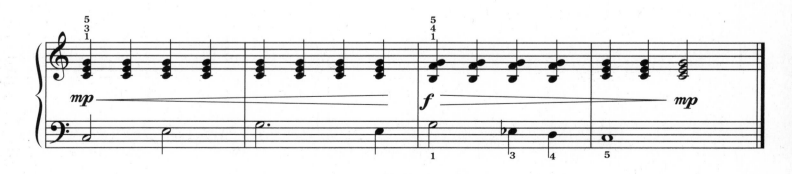

Theme from a Mozart Sonata

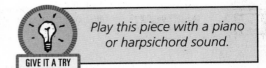

Play this piece with a piano or harpsichord sound.

Wolfgang Amadeus Mozart

MELODIC & HARMONIC 6THS

To play a 6th, skip four white keys.

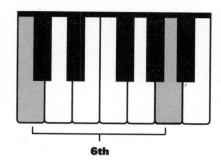

6th

Notice that 6ths are written **line to space** or **space to line**. To reach a 6th, you must reach one key further than a 5-finger position.

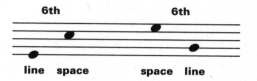

The F major and G7 and F chords both use 6ths.

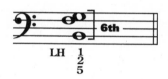

One 6th is labeled in the following piece; you label the rest.

Sixth Sense

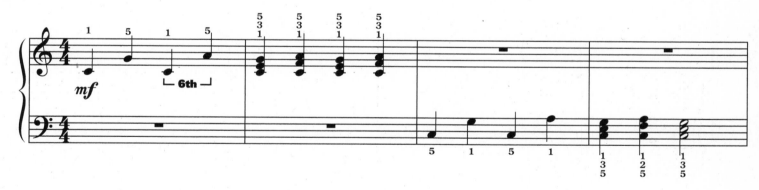

VIDEO EXAMPLE

MELODIC & HARMONIC 7THS

To play a 7th, skip five white keys.

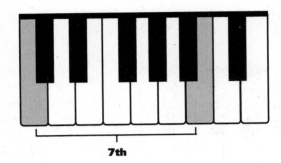

7th

Notice that 7ths are written **line to line** or **space to space**. A 7th spans all the letters of the music alphabet.

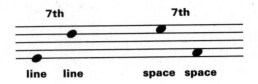

7th   7th

line   line   space   space

GIVE IT A TRY

One 7th is labeled in the following piece; you label the rest.

AUDIO EXAMPLE

Seventh Heaven

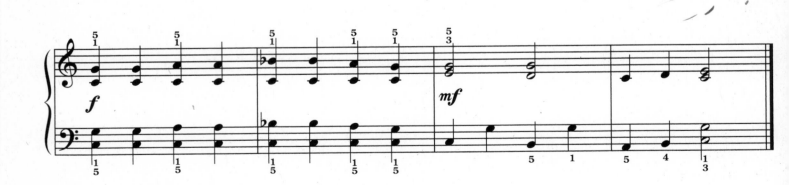

OCTAVES

You can think of an *octave* as an 8th, though it is never called that. An octave is easy to find because it is the distance from one note to the next note of the same name: C to C, D to D, etc.

To play an octave, skip six white keys.

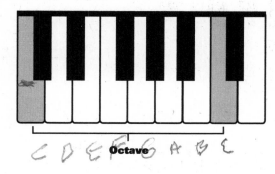

Notice that octaves are written **line to space** or **space to line**. The two notes of an octave always have the same name.

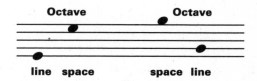

One octave is labeled in the following piece; you label the rest.

Octaboogie

HALF STEPS & WHOLE STEPS

Every piece of music is based on a particular set of notes called a *scale.* In order to understand how this works, we must understand the building blocks of the scale, namely, *whole steps* and *half steps.*

Half Steps

The smallest step is a *half step* (H), which is from one key to the very next key. Natural half steps occur between B & C and E & F; all other half steps are from a white key to a black key, so one of the notes will be a sharp or flat.

These are all half steps:

Whole Steps

A *whole step* (W) skips over one key. A whole step, in other words, is two half steps. Natural whole steps occur between any two white keys with a black key between them; all other whole steps will have at least one sharp or flat note.

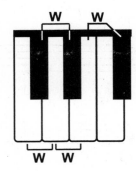

These are all whole steps:

THE KEY OF C MAJOR

The *major scale* is a set of eight notes that follow the pattern W-W-H-W-W-W-H. Each note of the scale is given a number, called a *degree*.

If you start on the note C and play all the white keys up to the next C, you've played the *C major scale:* C D E F G A B C.

C Major Scale

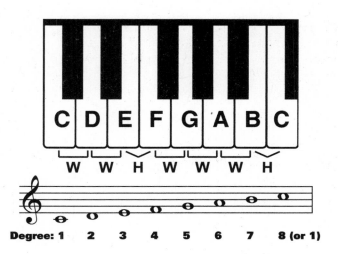

C Major Scale Split

In this exercise, the right hand plays some bass clef notes, and the left hand plays some treble clef notes.

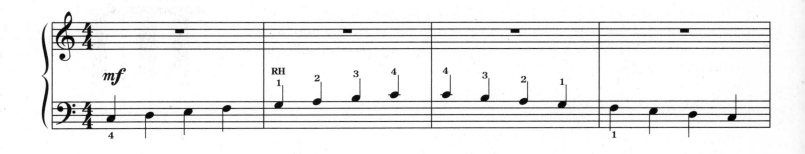

PRACTICING THE C MAJOR SCALE

Because there are eight notes in a scale and only five fingers on each hand, playing an entire scale with one hand requires two finger-crossing techniques that are very important to master.

Thumb Crossing Under

1. Put your right hand in middle C position (thumb on middle C).

2. Press and hold down E with your third finger.

3. As you continue to hold down E, slowly alternate playing C and F with your thumb, passing the thumb under your third finger for the F. It is very important that you **do not twist your wrist.** Keep your fingers curved and your palm open to form a "tunnel" for your thumb; point your thumb into the tunnel to play the F.

4. Perform the same exercise with the left hand in middle C position. Hold down A with your third finger and alternate playing C and G with your thumb, using the same technique described above.

Third Finger Crossing Over

1. Put your right hand in position with thumb on F.

2. Press and hold down F with your thumb.

3. As you continue to hold down F, slowly alternate playing A and E with your third finger, crossing your third finger over your thumb for the E. Again, it is extremely important not to twist your wrist. Use your thumb joint to pivot horizontally over to the E.

4. Perform the same exercise with the left hand in position with thumb on G. Hold down G with your thumb and alternate playing E and A with your third finger, using the same technique described above.

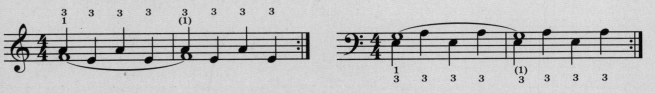

Now we'll put the whole thing together.

TEMPO MARKINGS

Tempo markings indicate how fast music is played. Like dynamics, many tempo marks are Italian words. Below are three of the most common Italian tempo markings.

Andante	(ahn-DAHN-teh)	slow
Moderato	(mod-deh-RAH-toh)	moderately
Allegro	(ah-LAY-groh)	fast

Scales are great for improving your technical agility. Practice the C major scale exercise below as a warm-up before your daily practice. Repeat the entire exercise three times at each of the indicated tempos. If the fingering is difficult when you play hands together, spend extra time practicing just that spot until it is easy, then go back and play the whole exercise from the beginning.

Note: On the DVD, the scale is played only once at each tempo.

C Major Scale Exercise

Andante (3 times)
Moderato (3 times)
Allegro (3 times)

ARTICULATION

Music notation uses a variety of symbols that tell the performer exactly how to play a piece of music so that it sounds as the composer intended. Dynamics and tempo markings, for example, tell how loud and how fast to play. Other symbols, called *articulations,* give even more specific instructions about how to play the notes. For example, notes can be played smoothly connected, like the calm flow of a river, or notes can be played separate and detached from one another, like the sound of falling raindrops. Articulations are details that give music life and character, so always follow them carefully.

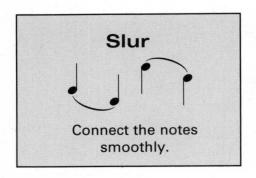

Slur

Connect the notes smoothly.

Staccato

Play the notes detached.

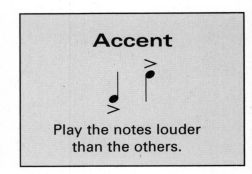

Accent

Play the notes louder than the others.

Note: Don't confuse a slur with a tie. A tie will always connect two of the same note, and a slur will connect two different notes *or* several notes together.

Slide, Bounce, and Bang

Be sure to play all the slurs, staccatos, and accents correctly.
Try to play them correctly even the first time you practice the piece.

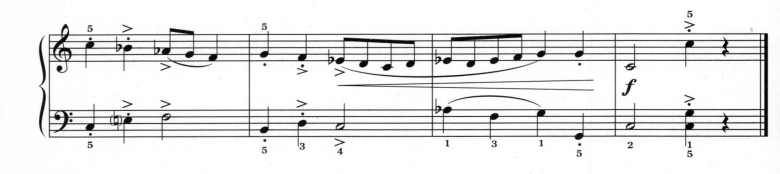

RITARDANDOS & FERMATAS

The marking *ritardando* means to gradually slow down. The direction *a tempo* tells you to return to the normal tempo. It is important to slow down gradually for a ritardando rather than simply becoming suddenly slower. Think of it as a car coming gradually to a stop rather than a car hitting a brick wall.

rit. or *ritard.*	gradually slower
a tempo	return to the normal tempo

A *fermata* means to pause. Notes with a fermata should be held about twice as long as normal.

Fermata

Pause (hold about twice as long).

Good Morning to You

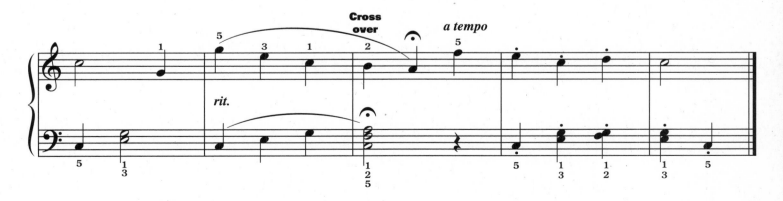

2/4 TIME SIGNATURE

2 A **2** means there are **two** beats in each measure.

4 A **4** means a **quarter note** ♩ gets one beat.

Russian Folk Dance

The two-note slur with a staccato has a characteristic "down-up" sound. This is accomplished by allowing the wrist to dip loosely for the first note, then lift up for the second note. Be sure to keep the wrist relaxed.

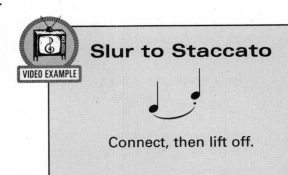

Slur to Staccato

Connect, then lift off.

Ludwig van Beethoven

Moderato

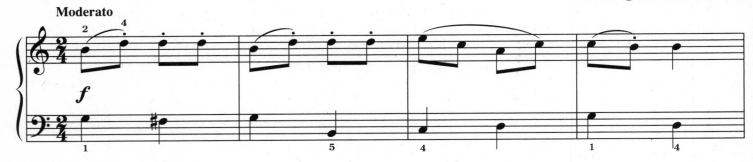

Cross over

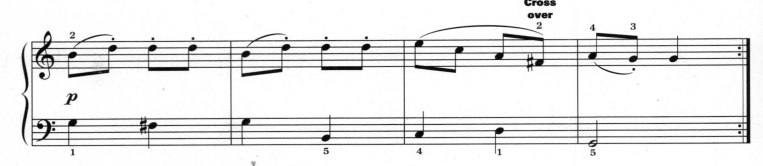

When you get to the end, repeat from here, not the beginning.

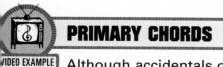

PRIMARY CHORDS

Although accidentals occur frequently in music, most pieces stick to the notes of one particular scale, which gives the music a sense of unity and direction. This concept of a scale providing a sort of musical "home base" is known as being *in a key*. For example, a piece that is composed using the C major scale is in the *key of C major*.

As you know, a *chord* is a combination of three or more notes played together. You also learned that the *root* of a chord is the note that gives the chord its name; C is the root of a C major chord, F is the root of an F major chord, and so on.

Triads

A *triad* is a chord with three notes: the root, a third above the root, and a fifth above the root. Let's take a look at the triads that can be formed using each note of the C major scale as a root.

In the diagram below, a triad has been built on each degree of the scale. Three of these triads, those built on the 1st, 4th, and 5th degrees of the scale (see page 63), are especially important and are called the *primary triads*. Notice the Roman numerals below the corresponding scale degree numbers—these can be used to refer to the chords of the scale. For example, the triad built on the 1st degree is called the I chord ("one" chord), the triad built on the 4th degree is the IV chord ("four" chord), and the triad on the 5th degree is the V chord ("five" chord). The primary triads, I, IV & V, are the three most functional, or useful, chords in any key. In the key of C, the primary chords are C major, F major, and G major.

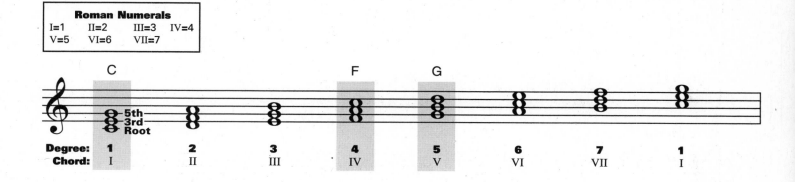

The arrangement of chords in a particular order is called a *progression*. Play the example below and listen carefully. As you hold the notes of the V chord, try to imagine what the I chord will sound like. It sounds like the music wants to return to the I chord in order to be finished.

Primary Progression

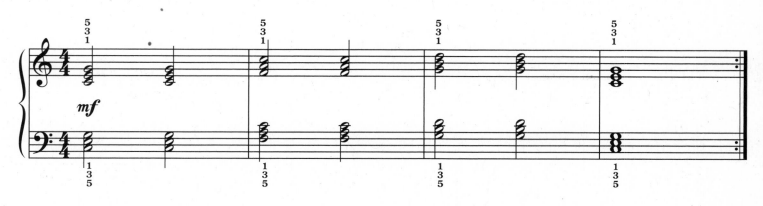

CHORD INVERSIONS

Let's take a look at how the familiar inversions of the chords you already know are derived.

The C, F, and G major triads on the previous page are in *root position*, meaning the root note is the lowest note of the chord. Earlier, you learned an inversion of the F chord (page 50) and an inversion of a type of G chord called a G⁷ chord (page 48). Where does the "7" come from in a G⁷ chord? It is simply an added note, an interval of a 7th above the root. The complete G⁷ chord, then, actually has four notes, though often only the root, 3rd, and 7th are played.

Primary Chords in the Key of C Major

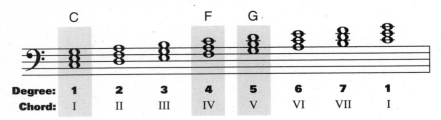 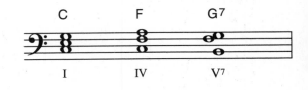

The following example features the primary chords in root position, followed by the same progression using inversions. Notice how the inversions make the progression easier to play on the keyboard.

Solid State

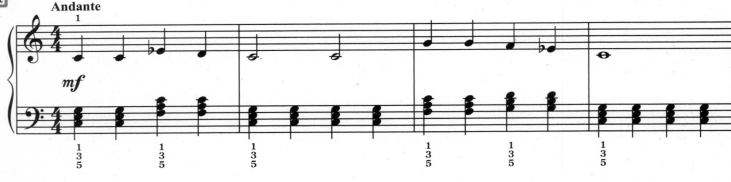

THE SUSTAIN PEDAL (DAMPER PEDAL)

Most pianos have two or three pedals. The pedal on the far right is the *damper pedal*, which, when depressed, lifts all the felt dampers off of the piano strings to allow the notes to ring. Electronic keyboards are typically equipped with a *sustain pedal* that creates the same effect as the piano's damper pedal. (The term "sustain pedal" will be used in this book to mean either pedal.)

Using the sustain pedal can add color and life to keyboard music. When pressed down, the pedal is "on." Because the notes continue to ring after you've lifted your fingers off the keys, it becomes possible to create a rich wash of harmony. To turn the pedal "off" and silence the notes, simply lift it up. Turning the pedal off and then immediately back on again is called *changing* the pedal. When playing music with sustain pedal, it is important to change the pedal appropriately in order to avoid creating a muddy mess of notes that aren't supposed to be heard at the same time. Always use your ears to be sure you aren't overdoing it.

In classical keyboard music, pedal markings are usually very specific and indicate exactly when to depress and release, as shown in the example below.

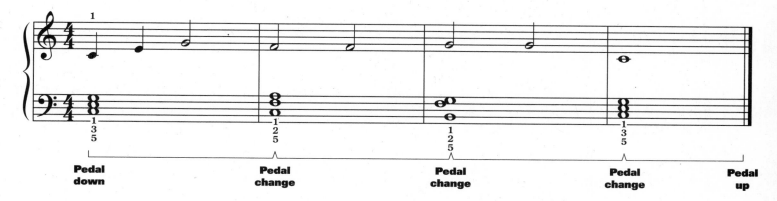

Sometimes, the abbreviation ℘. is used to show where the pedal should be pressed or changed. In this case, the symbol ✳ is used whenever the pedal should be taken off completely.

Important: In a lot of keyboard music, especially popular music, specific pedal on and off markings are not shown. Instead, the words "with pedal" might be seen under the first measure. In many cases, no indication whatsoever will be given; this does not necessarily mean pedal should not be used—it is simply being left to the discretion of the performer. Use your ears to decide what is best. (Hint: In most cases, you will want to change the pedal at least at the start of each measure.)

Bach Prelude in C

This famous prelude was used by Charles Gounod as the basis for the famous Bach/Gounod "Ave Maria." Follow the pedal markings carefully.

Johann Sebastian Bach

THE KEY OF G MAJOR

The G major scale contains one sharp, F♯. A piece of music based on the G major scale is said to be in the *key of G major.*

G Major Scale

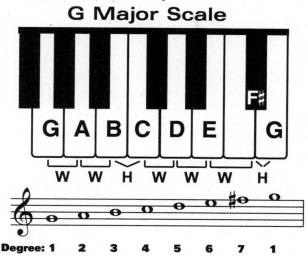

Degree: 1 2 3 4 5 6 7 1

G Major Scale

Practice the G major scale right hand alone, then left hand alone, then hands together three times at each of the indicated tempos. The fingering is the same as for the C major scale.

Note: On the DVD, the scale is played only once at each tempo.

Andante (RH, LH, together 3 times)
Moderato (RH, LH, together 3 times)
Allegro (RH, LH, together 3 times)

Primary Chords in the Key of G Major

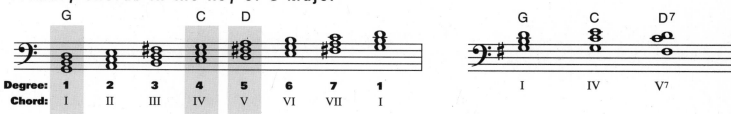

| Degree: | 1 | 2 | 3 | 4 | 5 | 6 | 7 | 1 |
| Chord: | I | II | III | IV | V | VI | VII | I |

74

VIDEO EXAMPLE

THE KEY SIGNATURE

A *key signature* indicates notes that will be sharp or flat throughout a piece of music. For example, music in the key of G major contains F♯. Rather than using accidentals to change all the F's in the music to F♯'s, the sharp can be placed in the key signature at the beginning of every staff.

Key Signature of G Major

Both lines of "All Through the Night" below will sound exactly alike.
Line 1 uses accidentals, and Line 2 uses a key signature.

AUDIO EXAMPLE

All Through the Night

Line 1

Line 2

Minuet in G

Notice the key signature! Play every F as an F#.

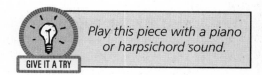

Play this piece with a piano or harpsichord sound.

Johann Sebastian Bach

Cross over just
for this note

A PIECE IN TWO KEYS

Here is a tune by Leopold Mozart, the father of Wolfgang Amadeus Mozart.
It is first shown in the key of C major, then in the key of G major. Playing the
same music in a different key is called *transposing*.

Burleske

Leopold Mozart

Key of C

Key of G

Alouette

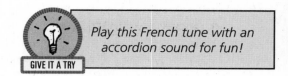

French folk song

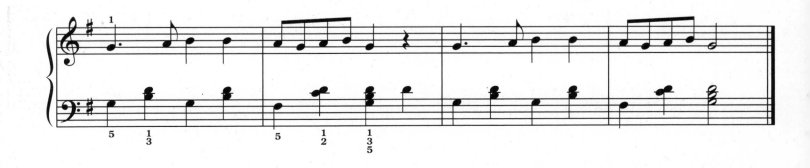

VIDEO EXAMPLE

TEMPO & EXPRESSION

Tempo markings, dynamics, and other changes in music create *expression*. Like dynamic signs, many tempo marks and other musical directions are Italian words.

Below are the most common Italian tempo markings and their meanings. Be sure to memorize them.

Largo	(LAHR-goh)	Very slow
Adagio	(ah-DAH-joh)	Slow
Andante	(ahn-DAHN-teh)	Moderately slow, walking speed
Moderato	(moh-deh-RAH-toh)	Moderately
Allegretto	(ahl-leh-GREH-toh)	Moderately fast
Allegro	(ahl-LAY-groh)	Fast
Presto	(PRES-toh)	Very fast

Other Italian words are often used to further indicate tempo, character, or feeling. Here are some of the more common ones you might see.

dolce	(DOHL-cheh)	Sweetly
subito	(SOO-bee-toh)	Suddenly, as in *subito p* (suddenly soft)
legato	(leh-GAH-toh)	Smooth
staccato	(stah-KAH-toh)	Detached
marcato	(mar-KAH-toh)	Heavily accented (sometimes indicated by the symbol ʌ)
molto	(MOHL-toh)	Very, as in *molto legato* (very smooth)
poco	(POH-koh)	Little, as in *poco dim.* (little diminuendo)
simile	(SEE-mee-leh)	In the same manner, as in *pedal simile* (continue the same pedal pattern)

Here's a handy chart of dynamic signs. Some you already know, others are new.

ppp	pianississimo	(pyah-nees-SEES-see-moh)	Very, very soft
pp	pianissimo	(pyah-NEES-see-moh)	Very soft
p	piano	(PYAH-noh)	Soft
mp	mezzo piano	(MED-zoh PYAH-noh)	Moderately soft
mf	mezzo forte	(MED-zoh FOHR-teh)	Moderately loud
f	forte	(FOHR-teh)	Loud
ff	fortissimo	(fohr-TEES-see-moh)	Very loud
fff	fortississimo	(fohr-tees-SEES-see-moh)	Very, very loud

TIPS

Remember: The more expression you put into your playing, the more skilled you will sound as a performer. So follow all the signs and symbols in the written music!

TRIPLETS

A *triplet* is three notes played in the time of two. An eighth-note triplet is three eighth notes played in one beat. The notes of an eighth-note triplet appear beamed together with a small number 3.

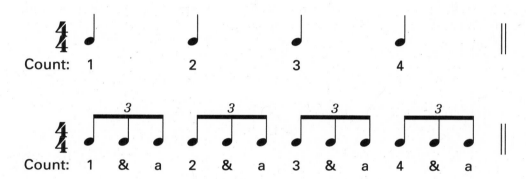

Beautiful Dreamer

Count carefully!

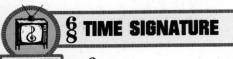

In $\frac{6}{8}$ time, the eighth note, not the quarter note, receives one beat.

A **6** means there are **six** beats in each measure.

An **8** means an **eighth note** ♪ gets one beat.

Note Values in $\frac{6}{8}$ Time

♪ = 1 beat   ♩ = 2 beats   ♩. = 3 beats   𝅗𝅥. = 6 beats

Music in this time signature is felt with two strong pulses: on beat 1 and beat 4.
Below are some common rhythmic groupings.

Alphabeats

The Irish Washerwoman

Traditional Irish tune

THE KEY OF F MAJOR

The F major scale contains one flat, B♭. A piece of music based on the F major scale is said to be in the *key of F major.*

F Major Scale

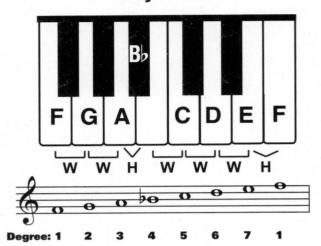

Key Signature of F Major

F Major Scale

Notice the different fingering in the right hand. Because of the placement of the black key in the scale, the thumb must cross under the fourth finger rather than the third finger. Remember to play every B as B♭ because of the key signature.

Note: On the DVD, the scale is played only once at each tempo.

Andante (RH, LH, together 3 times)
Moderato (RH, LH, together 3 times)
Allegro (RH, LH, together 3 times)

Primary Chords in the Key of F Major

AUDIO EXAMPLE

Joy to the World

Follow all the dynamics and articulations to make this holiday
favorite fun and exciting! Remember to observe the key signature.

Try playing with a
festive brass sound!

GIVE IT A TRY

Traditional

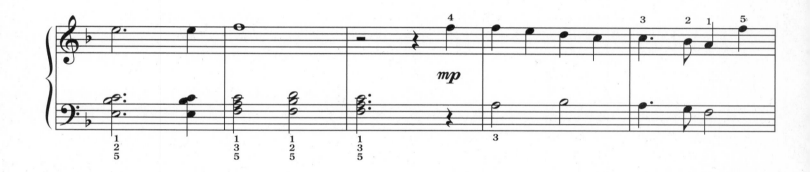

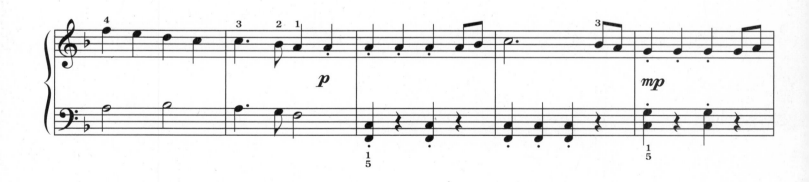

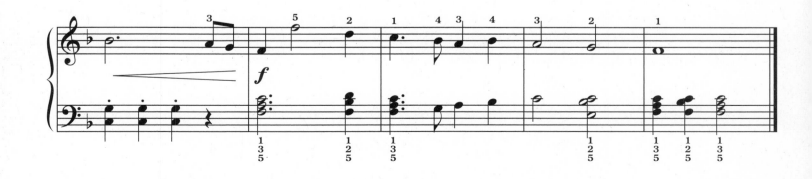

A PIECE IN THREE KEYS

Here we have a tune written in each of the three keys
you've learned: C, G, and F. Follow the key signatures.

Three-Key Rock

Key of C

Key of G

Key of F

REPEATS

In music notation, there are several ways to show when some or all of the music should simply be repeated the same way. You have already learned about repeat dots, which tell you to go back to the beginning of the music or back to repeat dots facing the other way. Here are some of the more elaborate repeat signs.

1st and 2nd Endings
On the repeat, skip the 1st ending and play the 2nd ending instead.

Ode to Joy (Beethoven)

D.C. al Fine
D.C. stands for *da capo*, which means the beginning. *Fine* means the end.
When you see D.C. al Fine, go back to the beginning and play to the *Fine* sign.

Au Claire de la Lune (French folk tune)

D.S. al Fine
D.S. stands for *dal segno*, which refers to the sign 𝄋.

When you see D.S. al Fine, go back to the 𝄋 and play to the *Fine* sign.

The Marines' Hymn (U.S. Marine Corps)

MINOR KEYS

A *minor* sound has a different quality than a *major* sound. Minor sounds are often considered dark, moody, or somber, whereas major sounds have a bright and cheerful feel.

For every major scale, there is a *minor* scale that contains the same notes and therefore uses the same key signature. The notes of the minor scale can be played by starting and ending on the sixth degree of a major scale. For example, playing all the white keys from C to C is a C major scale, but starting and ending on A gives you the A minor scale. Because of its close relationship to the major scale, it is known as the *relative minor*.

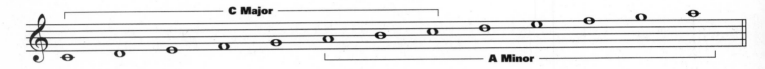

Below are the three major scales you know and their relative minor scales. These minor scales are known as *natural minor* because they contain the exact same notes as the relative major scale.

Practice these scales daily. Play the right hand alone, then left hand alone, then hands together three times Andante, then Moderato, then Allegro.

Major Scale

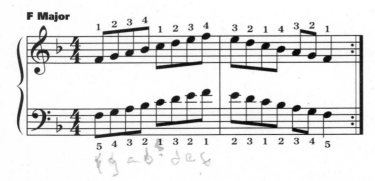

Relative Minor Scale

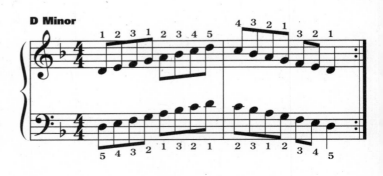

Scherzo

This example begins in A minor and then changes to the relative major, C.
Listen to how the character of the music changes.

Carl Maria von Weber

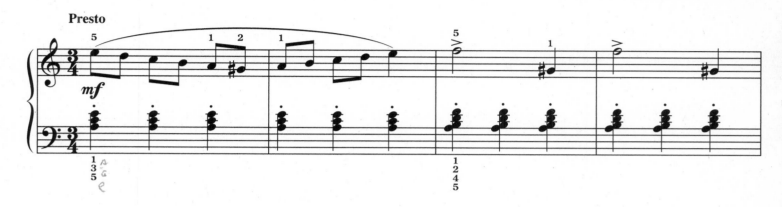

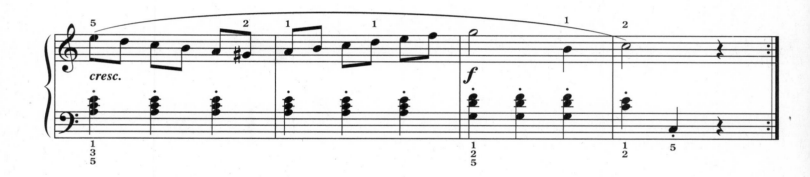

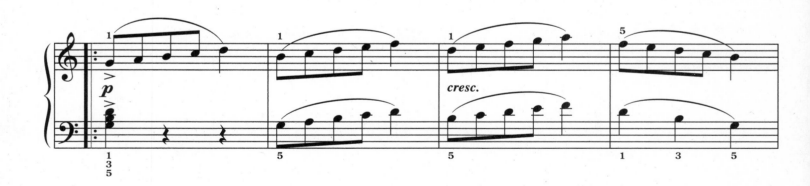

HARMONIC MINOR

VIDEO EXAMPLE

The *harmonic minor scale* is a form of the minor scale in which the seventh degree is raised a half step.

Below are the harmonic minor forms of the A minor, D minor, and E minor scales. Notice that the raised seventh step is written with an accidental and not put in the key signature.

GIVE IT A TRY

Practice these scales as the others, playing just right hand, then just left hand, then hands together, three times Andante, Moderato, then Allegro.

A Harmonic Minor

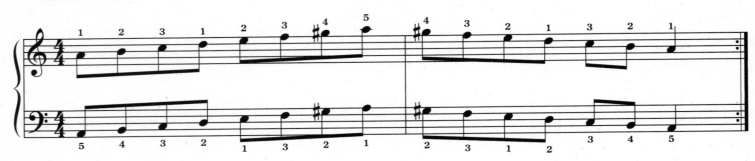

E Harmonic Minor

D Harmonic Minor

Primary Chords in Minor Keys

For music in a minor key, the chords are built using the notes of the harmonic minor scale. The concept is the same as for the major scale: the primary triads are I, IV, and V. The I and IV chords in a minor key are *minor triads.* The V chord is usually played as a V^7, just like in a major key.

Triads in A Minor

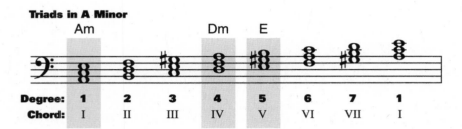

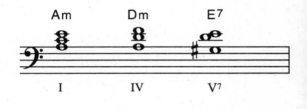

Triads in E Minor

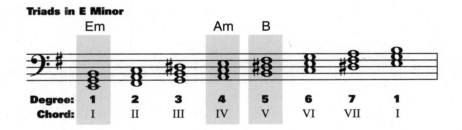

Triads in D Minor

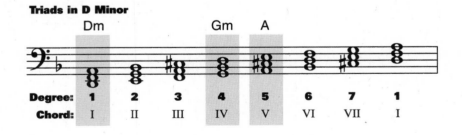

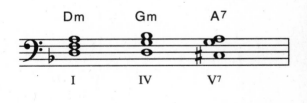

Symphony No. 40

A *coda* is an ending. When you see D.C. al Coda, go back to the beginning and play until you see *To Coda*, then skip to the coda marked by the symbol ⊕.

Notice the key signature: Does this piece sound like it is in G major, or the relative minor, E minor? (The answer is at the bottom.)

Wolfgang Amadeus Mozart

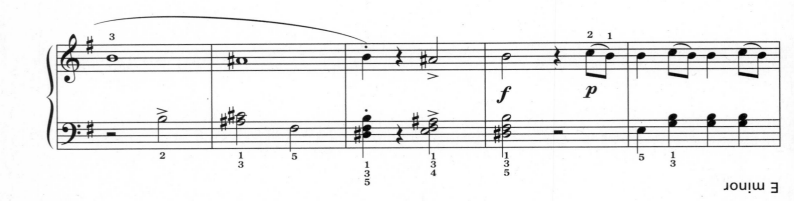

E minor

Waves of the Danube

Here's a piece with a key signature of one flat. Can you tell if it is F major or its relative minor, D minor? (The answer is at the bottom of the page.)

This tune is frequently played at anniversary celebrations.

Ion Ivanovici

D minor

The Entertainer

Congratulations! You're about to play an arrangement
of one of the most popular pieces of keyboard music
ever written. Be sure to follow all the dynamics and
articulations to make this ragtime classic come alive!

Play this Joplin favorite with a
honky-tonk piano sound!

GIVE IT A TRY

Scott Joplin

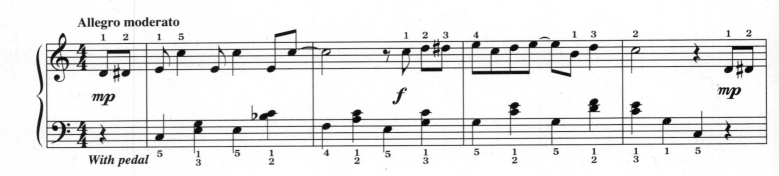

PART 2: ROCK

CHORDS

In this section of the book, you'll use the skills and knowledge you have gained so far and put them together with some important new concepts and techniques to start playing rock! You'll learn new chords, scales, rhythms, and bass lines. Also, you will learn how to solo using the pentatonic scale and the blues scale. Let's dig in and get started.

The Workhorse of Rock: The Triad

A *chord* is a group of three or more notes played together. A *triad* is a three-note chord. Most rock music uses triads. Triads are derived from the major scale, and are built with intervals of a 3rd. For example, if you play the root, 3rd and 5th of a C major scale, you will create the C major triad. It's that easy!

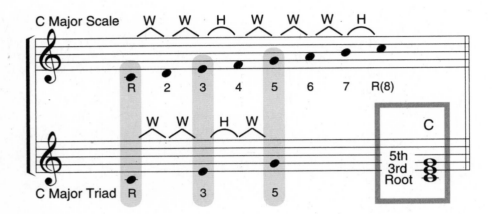

Let's check the intervals used in the C major triad (in rock lingo, we would simply say "C chord").

All major triads have the same formula of interval relationships:

1 = The Root.

3 = The middle note or 3rd of the chord (a major 3rd above the root).

5 = The upper note or 5th of the chord (a minor 3rd above the 3rd

or

a perfect 5th above the root).

We built our C chord on the root of a C major scale. We can build similar triads on the root of any major scale (see all the major scales starting on page 204). Let's build a few more chords. Notice how all major chords have the same formula.

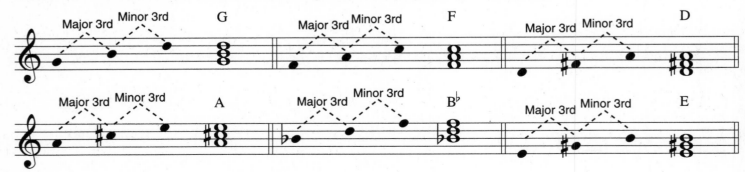

Here is a good exercise for learning the major chords. Learn it with your right hand and then with the left. The chord names are written above the music. Notice that chords with sharps in their names can also be called by their flat names. For example, C# can also be called D♭, A# can also be called B♭, and so on.

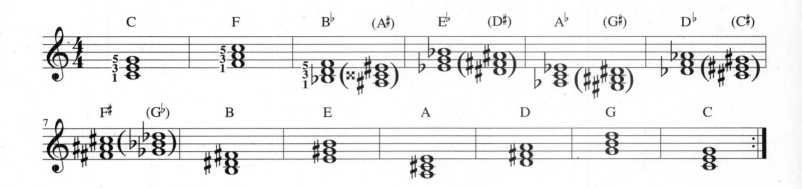

Here are the same chords played with the left hand.

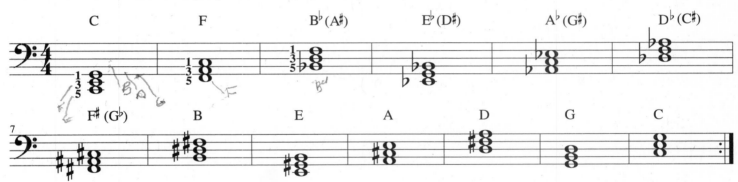

? DID YOU KNOW?

Booker T. Jones was the leader of Booker T. and the MGs who scored a major hit with Green Onions in 1962. They were responsible for creating the "Memphis Sound" and played on most of the big hits for Stax Records.

PHOTO • COURTESY OF THE ROSEBUD AGENCY

Here is a tune that uses major chords. The right hand plays mostly eighth-note triads and the left hand plays single notes. Follow the counting under the treble clef staff.

Babylon

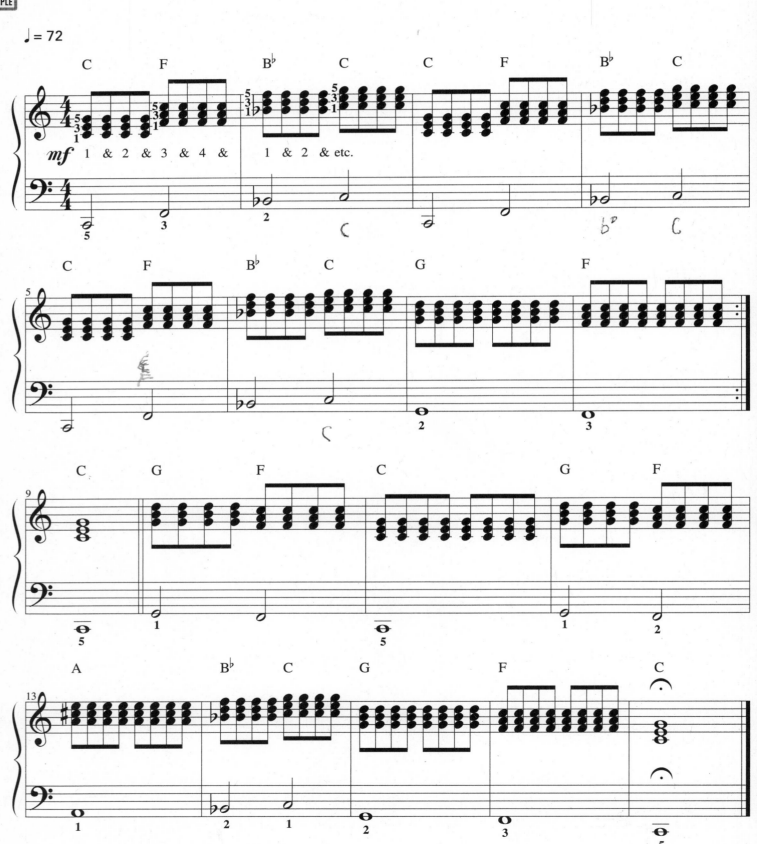

Minor Chords

Like major chords, minor chords are derived from scales. The formula for a minor triad is:

   1 = **The Root.**

   ♭3 = **The middle note or flat 3rd of the chord (a minor 3rd above the root).**

   5 = **The upper note or 5th of the chord (a major 3rd above the flat 3rd**
   or
   a perfect 5th above the root).

The example below shows how a minor triad can be derived from the 1st, 3rd and 5th degrees of a minor scale.

A Natural Minor Scale

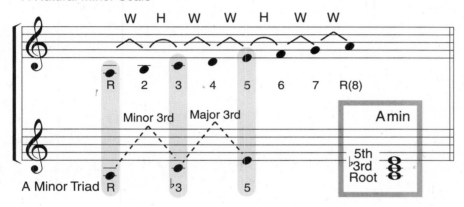

Below is an example comparing a C major chord with a C minor. Notice how the major triad can be made minor by lowering the 3rd. In sheet music, this chord is known as Cmin or Cm.

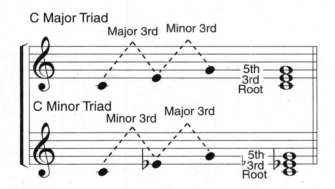

Here is an exercise to help you get acquainted with minor chords.

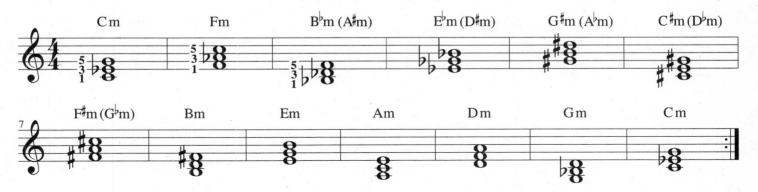

House of the Rising Sun is a traditional tune in the key of A minor. Notice that it includes the A minor chord. Eric Burden and the Animals recorded this song in the 1960s and it became an instant rock classic. Their arrangement featured a great rock keyboard part. In the arrangement provided here, the first section has the vocal melody in the right hand. The second section has chords in the right hand and a single-note bass line in the left.

This tune uses the $\frac{12}{8}$ time signature. There are twelve beats in each measure but we think of them in groups of three, with 1, 4, 7 and 10 being the "strong" beats (slightly accented). The result is really four beats per measure with each beat divided into three eighth notes (count 1-&-ah, 2-&-ah, etc.). This is called a *compound meter*. Four beats per measure with each beat divided into two eighth notes, $\frac{4}{4}$, is called a *simple meter*.

 Here is how the rhythm to this song is counted:

Rhythm Example

1 & ah 2 & ah 3 & ah 4 & ah

HOUSE OF THE RISING SUN

Major and Dominant 7th Chords

Most early rock tunes use simple major and minor triads. But occasionally rock players will use 7th chords to really make the tunes "sizzle"! A 7th chord is a four-note chord. If you take a triad and add a tone a 7th up from the root, you have a 7th chord. You can also think of it as adding another 3rd above the 5th of a triad.

Let's look at a C major triad with a 7th added above the 5th.

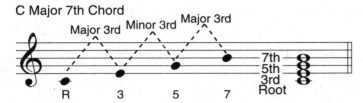

In sheet music, this chord is known as **CM⁷.**

The example above demonstrates that if you use the 7th that occurs naturally in the major scale of the root of the chord (in this case, the C major scale), the 7th is a major 7th, forming a *major 7th chord*. The major 7th chord is an excellent, sweet-sounding chord. Once in a while we sneak it into rock tunes. Red Hot Chili Peppers use a major 7th in *Under The Bridge* with great effectiveness.

In rock, the bluesy sounding *dominant 7th chord* is more commonly used. This kind of 7th chord has a ♭7 or minor 7th—the 7th is lowered one half step. The example below shows the formula for this cool sounding chord. Play it loud. Dominant 7th chords rock!

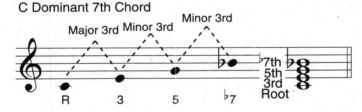

In sheet music, this chord is known as **C⁷.**

This exercise will give you some practice with dominant 7th chords. After you play it with the right hand, play it an octave lower with the left.

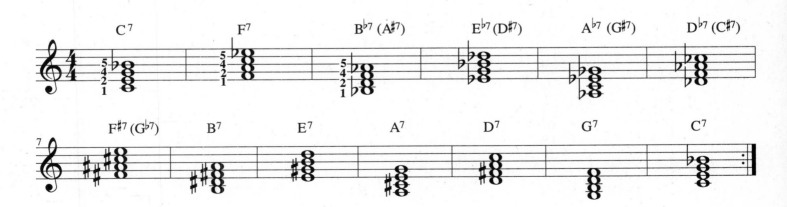

Let's play a tune using dominant 7th chords.

First Call

(*Last time only)

DID YOU KNOW?

Steve Winwood became famous in 1967 as the singer and keyboard player for the Spencer Davis Group. He later formed the group Traffic and became a very successful solo artist in the 1980s and 1990s.

Minor 7th Chords

Just as we add a ♭7 to a major chord to create a dominant 7th chord, we can add a ♭7 to a minor chord to create the four-note minor 7th chord. The example below shows the formula for a minor 7th chord.

C Minor 7th Chord

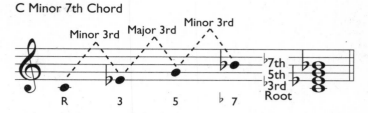

In sheet music, this chord is known as **Cmin7 or Cm7.**

This exercise will give you some practice with minor 7th chords. After you play it with the right hand, play it an octave lower with the left.

Here's a fun tune to play using minor 7th chords:

Isle of Dreams

AN INTRODUCTION TO ROCK RHYTHMS

The success of a good rock tune has a lot to do with strong rhythms. It doesn't take long to understand this concept if you hear a great live rock band pumping the music along at full tilt. The best of the bunch always have tremendous rhythms.

This style of music grew up in a time where unschooled or minimally trained musicians liberally borrowed the best rhythmic ideas from jazz, early blues and boogie-woogie. Boogie's repetitive bass lines were tossed into a stew with a dash of country simplicity making a rhythmic dish that became known as rock'n'roll. By pointing this musical feel at the emotions of the teens of the 1950s and '60s it became, and still is, one of the most popular musical styles ever.

You MUST get that rhythm thing happening to make it ROCK!

This is usually hashed out in the garages, rehearsal rooms and dance halls by bands trying to emulate their rock'n'roll heroes. But here are two secrets:

TIPS

#1. Make sure the time, or pulse, of the music is as steady as a ticking clock. Play along with your favorite recordings or use a metronome or similar device.

#2. Make sure everyone in your band feels the rhythm together. Listen carefully as you play.

Syncopation

Often, the difficulty in reading rhythms lies in the fact that music on the printed page *looks* harder than it actually is to play. This is because of *syncopation*. Syncopation is a shifting of the accent to a weak beat or weak part of a beat. In $\frac{4}{4}$ time, beats 1 and 3 are strong beats; beats 2 and 4 are weak. The *off-beats*—the "&s"—are the weak parts of the beats. The *on-beats*—where we count the numbers (1, 2, 3, 4)—are the strong parts of the beats.

To understand the concepts of off-beats and on-beats, you should study your feet. If you stomp your feet to the beat of a song with a steady rhythm, you learn that there are on-beats (when your foot is firmly planted on the floor) and off-beats (when your foot is lifted off the floor).

Here is a diagram of feet doing what they do to good rock music.

Tapping Your Feet

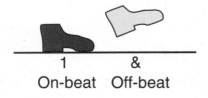

1 &
On-beat   Off-beat

No Syncopation

In this example, play a note on each on-beat. Keep the beat very steady.

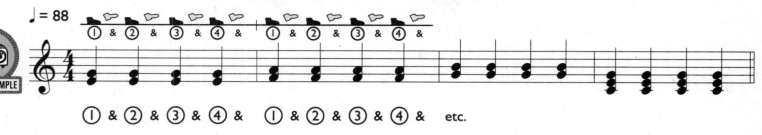

Good! But after awhile, rhythm like this can sound stiff. You may need more of that rock'n'roll, rhythmic punch.

Syncopated

This example includes a syncopation. The second accent is moved half a beat to the right of the second beat. The accents fall on beat 1 and the "&" of 2.

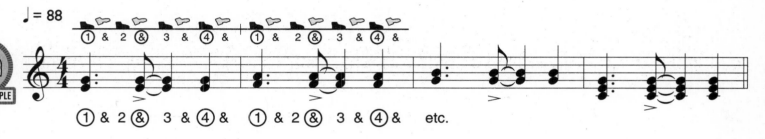

Use your metronome or drum machine. This will help you keep a steady tempo and make it easy to find the on-beats.

This seems simple enough. But syncopation often looks difficult on the printed page because it is frequently accomplished with ties. We read two notes when only one is sounded. If you write the beats under the music, it will be easier. As in the examples printed on this page, write the numbers with their "&" symbols (1 & 2 & 3 & 4 &). This will help you determine if you should play on a downbeat (1, 2, 3, 4) or an up-beat ("&"). You'll be rockin' in no time at all!

Syncopated with Ties

Here is another syncopated example using ties:

Rhythm Exercises
Bo Diddley
This example is in the style of Bo Diddley, a master of syncopated rhythms.

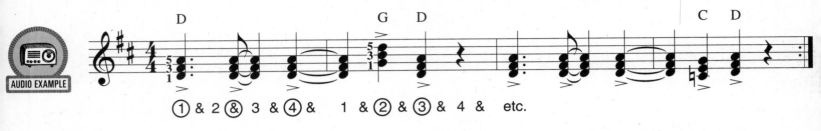

Dotted Notes and Ties
This example uses dotted notes and ties over the bar line to create syncopations.
Make sure the last F chord comes on beat 3. Avoid the tendency to lose track of
the on-beat when playing lots of off-beats.

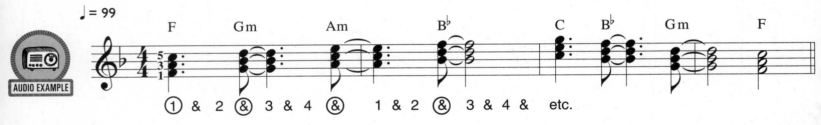

Straight Against Syncopated
Let's combine a straight quarter-note rhythm in the left hand with syncopations in
the right hand. Be careful to keep the left hand steady as you play the accents in
the right hand. One of the most important things to learn when playing keyboards
is independence between the hands.

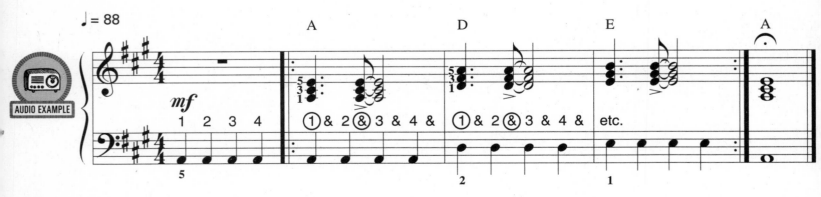

Rhythmic Independence

One of the important things a keyboardist must master is the ability to play two different rhythms simultaneously, one in the left hand and one in the right. Practice each tune very slowly, one hand at a time. Then, put the hands together, also very slowly, until each hand feels independent of the other. Finally, try a faster pace.

Over the Top

♩ = 104

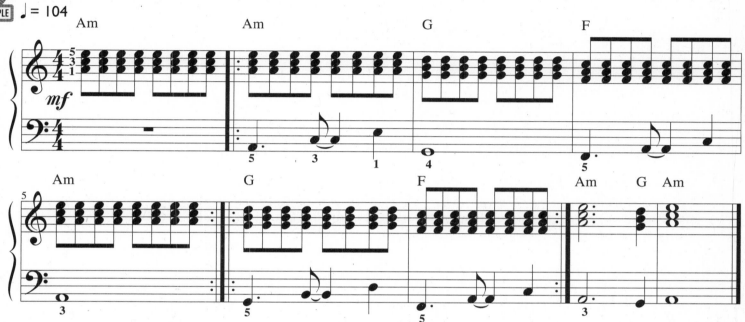

This exercise has syncopations in the right hand and steady eighth notes in the left.

Under the Depths

♩ = 104

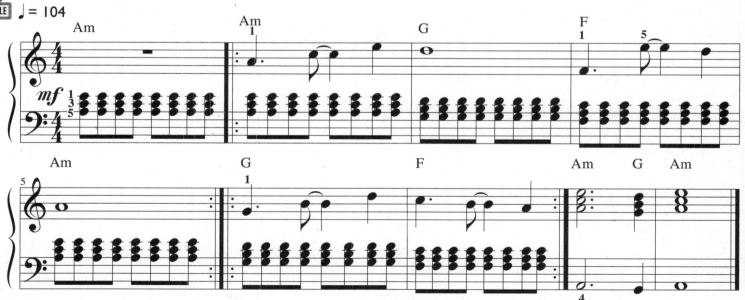

108

BASIC BASS LINES

> *It's the night of the big gig. You're on the bandstand, ready to rock out with your killer keyboard parts. Suddenly the band leader turns to you and says:*
>
> *"Bad news...the bass player's car broke down. He's stuck in the breakdown lane of the Jersey Turnpike. He's not gonna make it tonight. Your left hand is the bass player now. Good luck!"*
>
> *At this point, you either break into a cold sweat and run out of the room screaming, or you open your massive mental file of cool bass lines and say, "Let's rock!"*

Rock music always has strong bass lines. In the early days of rock'n'roll, pianists like Jerry Lee Lewis and Fats Domino played hard rockin' left-hand bass lines—often borrowed from barrelhouse or boogie-woogie piano—that vigorously drove the music forward.

A rock keyboardist might be called upon to double the bass guitar part for an even more solid bottom-end sound. The Doors, the legendary 1960s act led by Jim Morrison, never had a bass player in concert. Ray Manzarek's left hand on a Fender keyboard bass provided their bass. As the scenario above suggests, you may have to play bass on a synthesizer or keyboard sampler someday, so let's learn some left-hand patterns.

The simplest left-hand part might be just holding the left hand in whole or half notes while the right hand plays the chords (see *Babylon* on page 98). It's more likely, however, that you'll need to lay down some rockin' rhythms. Here are a few classic patterns. Count carefully to master the syncopated rhythms.

Let's put some of those patterns together in a song.

Get 'Em Up

♩= 110

ARPEGGIOS AND CHORD INVERSIONS

Arpeggios are broken chords. On the keyboard, this is a simple matter of playing chords in varying patterns, up and down, mostly one note at a time.

Here are some common arpeggio patterns. Play these with the right hand and then an octave lower with the left hand.

Notice that the next example is written in bass clef, for the left hand. Also play it an octave higher with the right hand.

Play this with the right hand and then an octave lower with the left hand.

You first learned *House of the Rising Sun* on page 100. Here's your old friend back again, this time as an *accompaniment*, or backing part, with arpeggios.

House of the Rising Sun: Arpeggios

♩ = 63

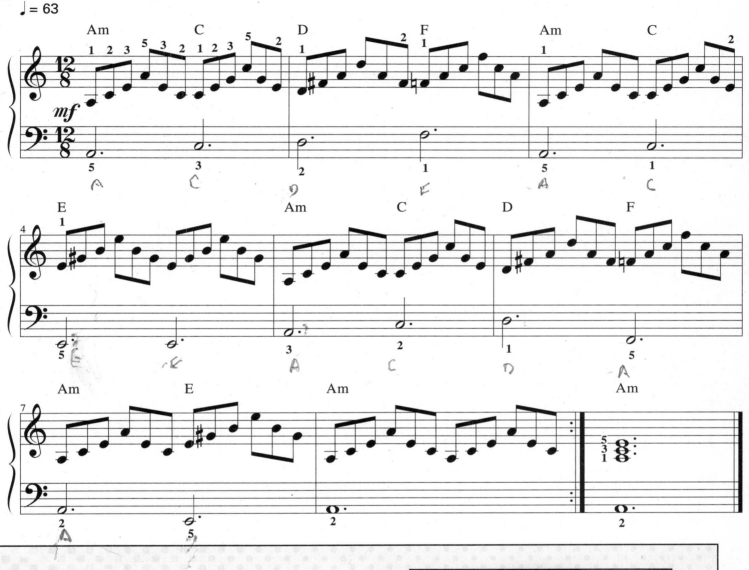

Billy Preston was a brilliant keyboardist who became an unofficial member of the Beatles in 1969, performing with them on their "Let It Be" album. In the 1970s, he became a very successful solo artist and had several hit records. In addition, performed with artists such as Ringo Starr and the Rolling Stones.

Chord Inversions

So far in this book, we've played most of our chords in *root position*. In other words, the root is the lowest note of the chord. But as you have seen, chords are often *inverted*. When a chord is inverted, something other than the root is the lowest note.

If the 3rd of the chord is on the bottom, it is said to be in *1st inversion*.

If the 5th of that chord is on the bottom, it is said to be in *2nd inversion*.

We have good reasons for using inversions:

1) To make the chord easier to finger and make smoother changes from one chord to another.

2) To make the chord sound higher or lower without going into the next octave.

3) To make smooth bass lines.

Here are four different major chords and their inversions:

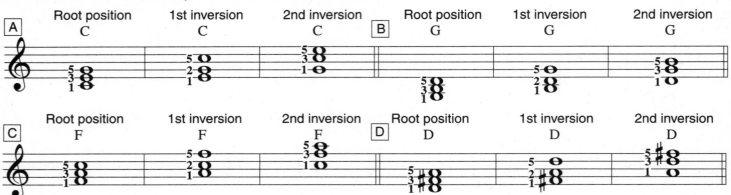

Minor chords are inverted in exactly the same way. Here are two different minor chords and their inversions:

The lowest note of the chord always determines the inversion, even if the lowest note is in the left hand. We can play an inversion with the right hand, but it is not truly an inversion if the left hand is playing the root. Below are a few inversions for both hands. Notice that a triad can be spread out so that the three notes are split up between the hands. Furthermore, it is important to note that the left hand is often doubling a note that is also being played in the right hand. Virtually any combination of the chord tones is possible, although some may be more desirable than others. In the end, your ear will be your guide. This important aspect of music is called *voicing*.

Slash Chords

In rock music, you will often see chord symbols with a slash (C/G, Dmin/C, F/D, etc.). A slash chord tells you there is an inversion lurking about. For instance, C/E tells you there is a 1st inversion C chord. C is the chord name and the lowest note is an E. The E is the 3rd of the chord.

Slash chords can aid in building totally different and interesting harmonies. For instance, C/D is a C chord with a D in the bass. The D is not a chord tone, so it makes for an interesting, colorful chord.

You will find that many inversions feel easier to play than the same chord in root position. Here is a tune you learned on page 98 but arranged here to include inverted chords.

In slash chords, the letter before the slash is the chord and the letter after the slash is the bass note.

C/D
Chord   Bass Note

Back to Babylon

♩ = 92

Better Voice Leading Through Inversions

Below are two versions of the same chord pattern. The first version uses all root position chords in the right hand. The second version uses mostly inverted chords in the right hand. The left-hand part is identical in both. It is possible that one might prefer the first version in some cases, but the second version is easier to play and smoother sounding. Each note of each chord moves more smoothly to each note of the next chord. This is a great example of using inversions to create better *voice leading*.

All Root Position Chords

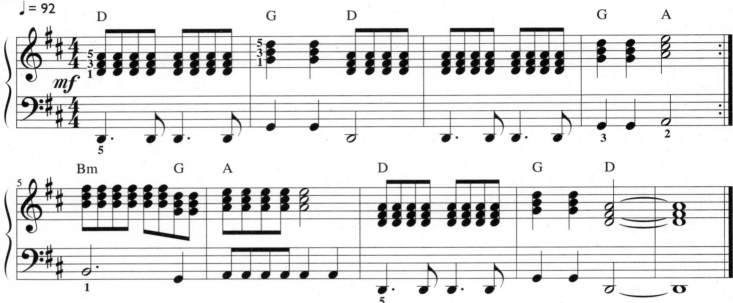

With Inversions for Better Voice Leading

7th Chord Inversions

Just as major and minor triads can be inverted, four-note 7th chords can be inverted. The difference is that since they have four notes, they can be inverted three times. The *3rd inversion* has the 7th as the lowest note of the chord.

Here are four different 7th chords with all three of their inversions. Notice how slash chords are used to indicate chord inversions.

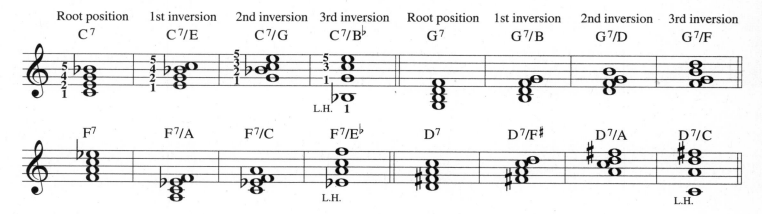

The same concept can be applied to minor 7th chords. Try lowering the 3rd of each 7th chord in the last example to create minor 7th chord inversions.

Down to Earth uses 7th chord inversions. Enjoy the rich sound of the chords. Notice the smooth, step-wise movement of the bass. This is a great reason for using inversions.

Have fun!

Down to Earth

♩ = 92

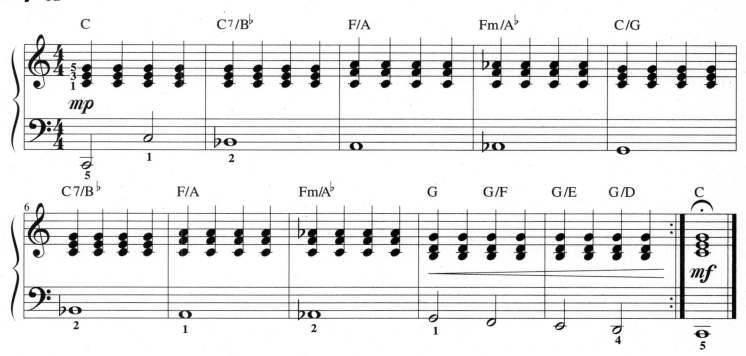

Pedal Tones

It is a common rock technique to change chords in the right hand while holding a single, unchanging note in the left hand. As the chords change, *dissonance* (a clashing sound) occurs causing tension and, often, suspense. The unchanging note in the left hand is called a *pedal tone*.

The term "pedal tone" is taken from an organ technique wherein the performer holds down a floor-pedal note with a foot, while playing a series of chords with the hands above the held note.

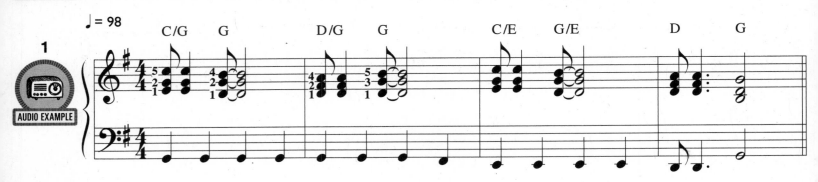

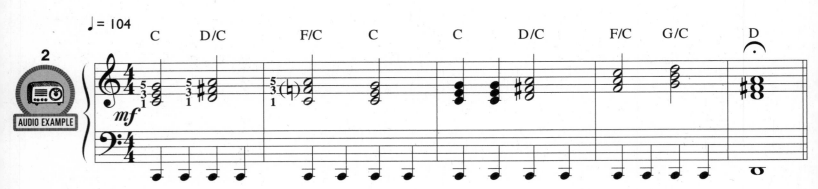

This one uses three different pedal tones.

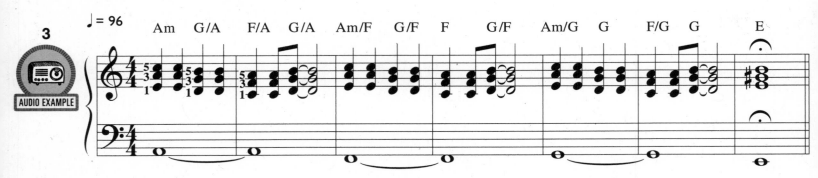

Here is a tune featuring pedal tones. Notice how the pedal tones are indicated in the slash chords; in the first four measures, there is almost always a "C" to the right of the slash.

Blue Fire

♩ = 112

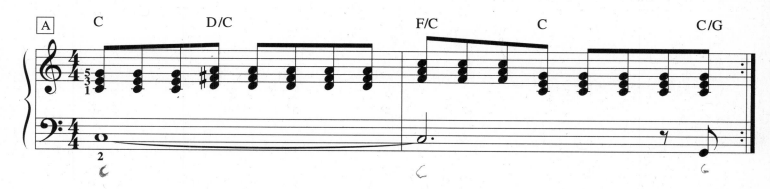

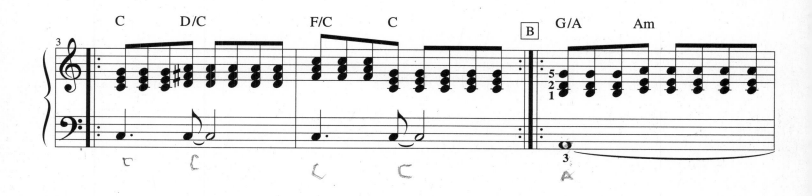

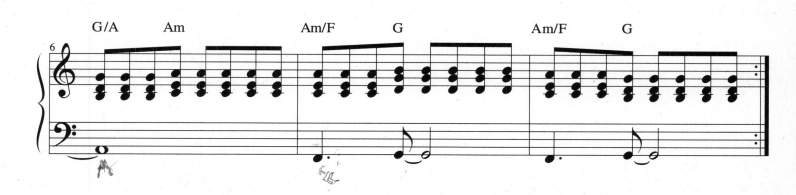

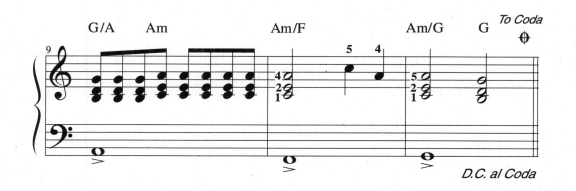

D.C. al Coda

READING A LEAD SHEET

Three Types of Lead Sheets

Sometimes rock music is written in a sort of rough sketch called a *lead sheet* (also called a *chart*). There are several kinds of lead sheets, and the type we use depends on the situation. Sometimes the melody is shown on a treble clef staff with lyrics below and chords above. Other times, the melody is ignored and just chords are written over slashes that show the number of beats per bar. Another kind of lead sheet shows the chords to play and *rhythmic notation* (a style of music notation that shows only the rhythm and not any specific pitch).

Below is an example of a lead sheet similar to what you might see in a collection of standard tunes. This is the melody-and-chord-only style lead sheet. If this were a true song, lyrics would be shown below the notes.

Here is the same music with slashes instead of the melody. The slashes designate the time in each bar and the player is free to make up a part using the chords above the staff.

The following lead sheet uses rhythmic notation. The player uses the rhythm shown as a guide to where accents should be placed. The diamond shapes and small slashes replace the standard note heads and their placement does not indicate any particular pitch. Stems, and sometimes flags and beams, give the rest of the rhythmic information.

Rhythmic Notation Basic Note Values

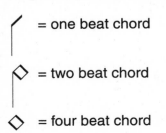

= one beat chord

= two beat chord

= four beat chord

Here is a simple realization of the first lead sheet on page 118 using just triads in the left hand.

This simple realization of our four-bar lead sheet would do in a pinch, but the left-hand part is somewhat stiff and muddy sounding. Since lead sheets almost never give the left-hand part, we are challenged to come up with a left-hand part that sounds good and moves the tune forward.

Here is a better suggestion for the left hand with the right hand playing the melody. The circled notes in the right hand are chord tones. This is a good example of how one hand can perform two functions at once: melody and accompaniment. Notice that the left-hand part is kept very simple. It provides a bass of roots and 5ths.

Lead sheets may not be the best way to write music but they are short and simple to read. They provide a good "roadmap" of where a song is going and allow you the freedom to create your own part. Because of its simplicity, a lead sheet can be an aide for memorizing songs, too.

Song Form Terminology

To understand song *forms* (the form is the organization of the song) and lead sheets, musicians use terms to describe different sections of a song.

The most common terms are: *intro, verse, chorus* and *bridge.*

The *intro* is the introduction or beginning of a song.
The *verse* is the part of the song that tells the story. Most songs have several verses.

The *chorus* is the part of the song that is repeated often and without variation. It summarizes or comments on the point of the story told in the verses.

The *bridge* is connecting musical material that is different from the verse and chorus. It adds a contrast to the verse and chorus.

USING LETTERS TO DESCRIBE SONG FORM
Here are two examples of how a song form can be described with letters.

Verse	Verse	Chorus	Verse	Chorus
A	A	B	A	B

Verse	Chorus	Verse	Chorus	Bridge	Chorus
A	B	A	B	C	B

Other terms you may see are *outro* or *tag* or *Coda.* These are just three different ways to say the same thing: the end of the song.

Three Charts

Here is an example of a more elaborate lead sheet.

Riding on the Wind: Melody Lead Sheet

The long line in the middle of the staff indicates more than one measure of rest. The number above the staff indicates how many measures of rest. The beginning of this song has two measures rest for the keyboard.

The lead sheet for "Riding on the Wind" shows why it is so important to understand how this style of notation works.

First, there is a two bar drum solo at the beginning. DON'T PLAY DURING THE DRUM SOLO. Drummers get upset if you steal their thunder, and they have hard objects in their hands.

The keyboard comes in at bar 3 and plays only chords up through bar 6.

The verse begins at bar 7. The singer, or lead instrument, would start there. The verse is played twice.

Then the band goes to the B section at measure 15, where the chorus begins.

After the chorus, there is one more verse and then another chorus.

After the last chorus, skip to the Coda and end the song.

Don't overlook the change of key signature from A minor in the verse to A major in the chorus.

The next lead sheet uses rhythmic notation. Often, when rehearsing with a band, you won't get as much information as given in the chart shown on page 120. Notice that ties and dots occur in rhythmic notation just as in standard notation.

When playing this chart for the first time, use simple triads in the right hand and single root notes in the left hand. As you become more familiar with the tune, add variations, such as inversions, to the right-hand part.

Riding on the Wind: Rhythmic Notation Lead Sheet

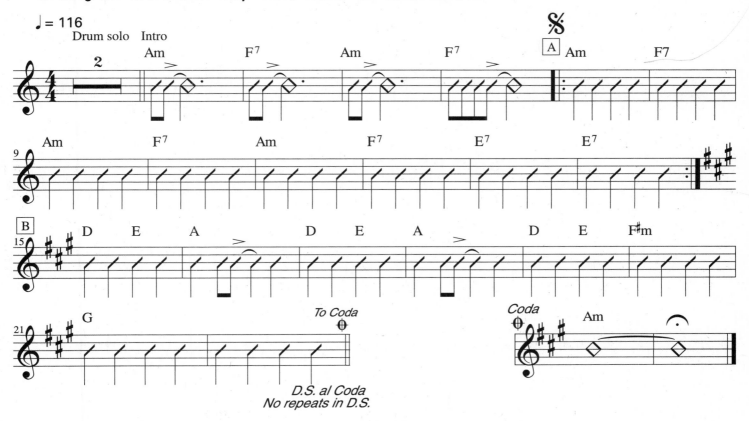

As with the previous chart, use simple triads in the right hand and single root notes in the left hand.

House of the Rising Sun: Chord and Slash Lead Sheet

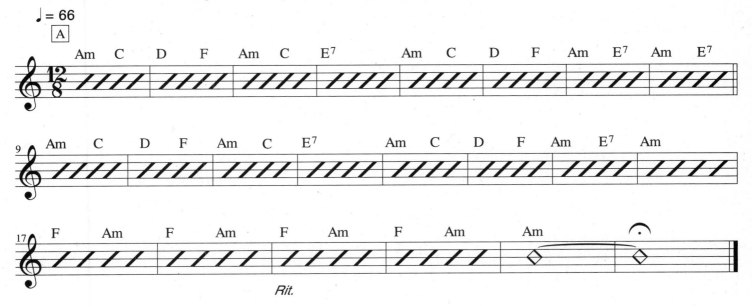

MORE LEFT-HAND PATTERNS

As you know, lead sheets deliberately leave out a left-hand part. Since we know that good rockin' piano needs a strong bass line, here are a few pages of left-hand patterns. They will come in handy when playing from lead sheets.

Boogie-Woogie Patterns

Boogie piano developed in the black urban centers as an outgrowth of the raucous barrelhouse piano of the early 20th century. This style relies on a strong percussive bass line to drive the songs forward and makes you want to move your feet.

Here is a classic left-hand line in quarter notes with the added 7th tone.

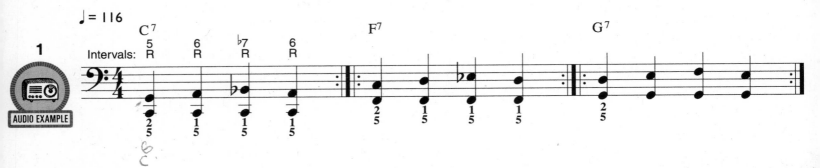

Here is another classic left-hand part. Guitar players are particularly fond of this idea, especially in the keys of A or E. On the keyboard, it's easiest in C.

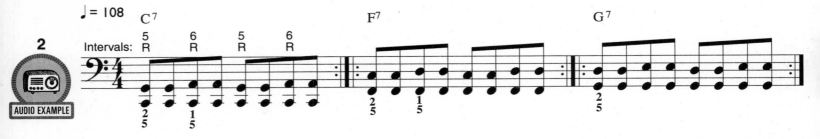

DID YOU KNOW?

Stevie Wonder was a Motown child prodigy who hit the top of the charts with *Fingertips (Pt. 2)* in 1963. He later matured into one of the most influential artists of the 20th century, recording most of the instruments on his dazzling solo albums.

Here is a boogie pattern in G. Strive to keep the pattern very steady with a solid feel. This pattern uses an A♯, which is the same as (enharmonically equivalent to) B♭. The B♭ is the ♭3, or minor 3rd, in G. This pattern highlights the sound of the minor 3rd moving to the major 3rd (B). This minor/major ambiguity is a big part of the language of blues- and boogie-influenced rock'n'roll.

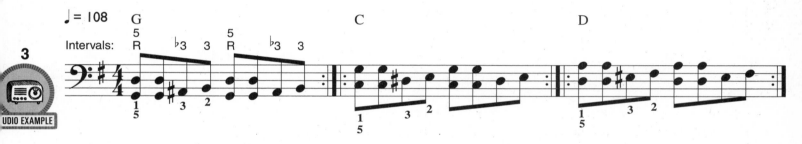

Here is a walking boogie bass line. Let's add a few chord hits to this next pattern. Learn the left hand first. As you add the right hand, keep the left hand very steady.

Walkin' & Talkin'

124

The pattern used in *This Rock'n'Roll Thing* will rock the house when played with spirit. Repeat the introduction until *you hit a groove* (where the rhythm starts to feel great!) and then add the right hand part. Pay attention to the first and second endings (see page 85).

This Rock'n'Roll Thing

♩= 124

= Repeat previous measure

Octaves

As you learned on page 61, an octave is the interval created between the two closest notes with the same letter name. It gets its name from the root *"oct"* which means "eight." The eighth note of a major scale is an octave above the root. An octave also equals twelve half steps. In keyboard music, octaves are often used to strengthen bass lines in the left hand. They are also used to add emphasis to a melody line in the right hand.

Octaves require extra effort and a little stretching of the fingers, especially for players with small hands. If your hands get tired, stop and rest. Some players have to "roll" their octaves—that is, play the lower note and then immediately jump to the higher note. Try playing a scale in octaves using one hand at a time.

1

Same fingering throughout.

2

Same fingering throughout.

Try an A major scale in the right hand.

3

Try a D major scale in the left hand.

4

126

Here are two tunes that feature octaves in the bass.

Miles From Nowhere

= Repeat previous two measures.

"Almost There" features the use of a *sus4 chord* in the 5th measure. In a sus4 chord, the middle note, or 3rd, is raised a half step to the 4th tone above the root. The 4th is called a "suspension" because in 14th century music, you could only get this sound by holding the note over, or suspending it, from a previous chord. In this case, the F#(3rd) of the D chord is raised to the G (4th) and suspended as an anticipation of the D chord in bar 6 where the 4th resolves down to the 3rd.

Almost There

Broken Octaves

Octaves can be used to make good, simple bass lines by alternating the pinky and thumb to create a rocking-back-and-forth motion in the left hand. Paul McCartney of The Beatles used this technique in songs such as *Lady Madonna* and *Martha, My Dear*.

Here are some rocking, broken-octave lines:

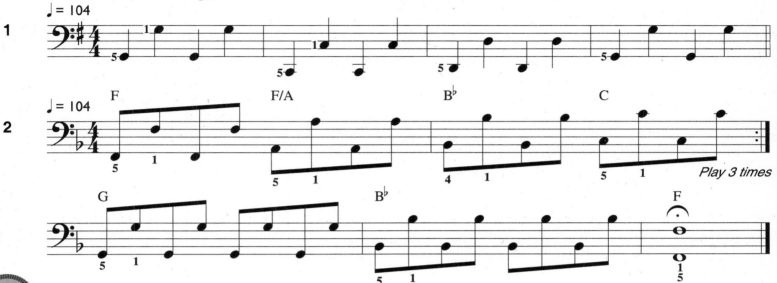

All Night Station

Play right hand second time only for both repeats.

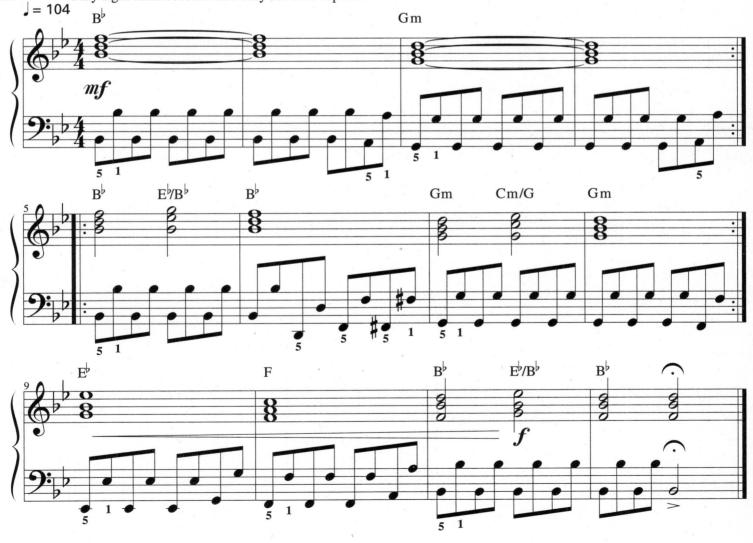

Boogie Lines in Octaves

Here is a classic boogie-woogie line with octaves.

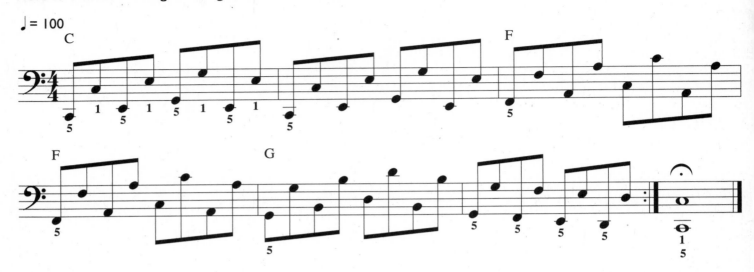

Billy Powell is one of the founding members of the Southern rock group, Lynyrd Skynyrd, which was established in the 1970s. His funky, rollicking piano style is an excellent compliment to their bluesy/country guitar leads.

DID YOU KNOW?

If it feels comfortable, you can try playing every other octave with a 4-1 fingering.
If you have an acoustic piano or full-size electric keyboard, play the left hand one
octave lower than written. Also, notice the key signature: four sharps! E major is
a big rock key. So, take it slow at first but get used to it! Rock on!

Saloon Spider

♩= 104

BEGINNING IMPROVISATION

Rock keyboard players are often part of the *rhythm section*—the group of instruments that accompany the singer or lead instrument. That is why we've concentrated on chords, left-hand bass lines and rhythms. But you may be called upon to take the lead melody or even *improvise* a solo! Improvising is the act of spontaneous invention. In music, that means creating music from your own imagination. If that sounds intimidating, don't panic. There are tools of the trade which make it simple. We'll start with the *pentatonic scales*.

Pentatonic Scales

When improvising, musicians often think about scales. We need to know which to use for soloing over the chords being played. Pentatonic scales are used in many rock tunes because they are simple and they fit like a glove over most basic chords.

Pentatonic scales are made up of five notes (*"penta"* is the Greek word for "five"). If you play just the black keys on the piano, you will have a pentatonic scale! (Notice that there are five black keys in every octave). Let's compare the now-familiar major scale with a *major pentatonic* scale.

Here are the C major and C major pentatonic scales:

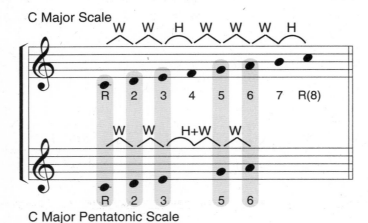

C Major Pentatonic Scale

The most tense notes in the major scale are the 4th (in the key of C, that's F) and the 7th (B). Play these notes against a C chord to hear why we think of them as tense. They are both dissonant (they clash) against the chord. The major pentatonic scale eliminates these notes. This is why the C major pentatonic scale fits so well with the C major chord.

The first time through *Deeper River*, play the C major pentatonic tune written out for the right hand. In the repeat, continue to play notes from the pentatonic scale randomly, and even in different octaves. The more you play, the easier it will become. Sometimes it helps to let two bars of left-hand accompaniment go by before beginning to improvise. This will help you solidify the left-hand part and get a feel for the rhythm.

GIVE IT A TRY

Try combining longer notes (quarter notes and half notes) with shorter notes (eighth notes) to create interesting rhythms for your improvisation.

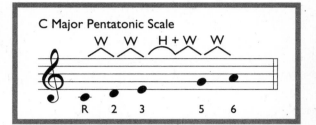

C Major Pentatonic Scale

W W H + W W

R 2 3 5 6

AUDIO EXAMPLE

Deeper River

♩ = 112

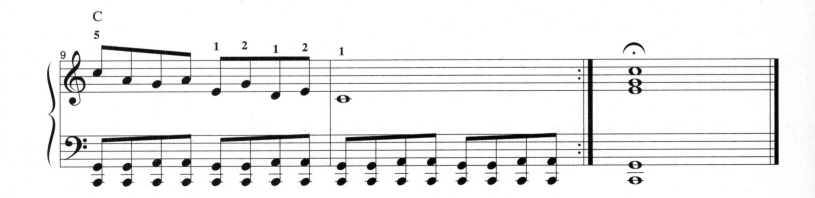

In the next example, the right hand plays three C major pentatonic *phrases*. A phrase is a complete musical thought. The music is like a little conversation, and the phrases are the sentences. Play the three written phrases and then improvise a fourth. Create a melody similar to the other three using the C major pentatonic scale. You get the last word in the conversation! Don't worry: you can play any note in the scale. There are no "wrong notes" as long as you stay in the scale. Experiment with different rhythms, and don't be afraid to leave a little space (rests) in your melody. If you have trouble being spontaneous, try writing a melody on the staff.

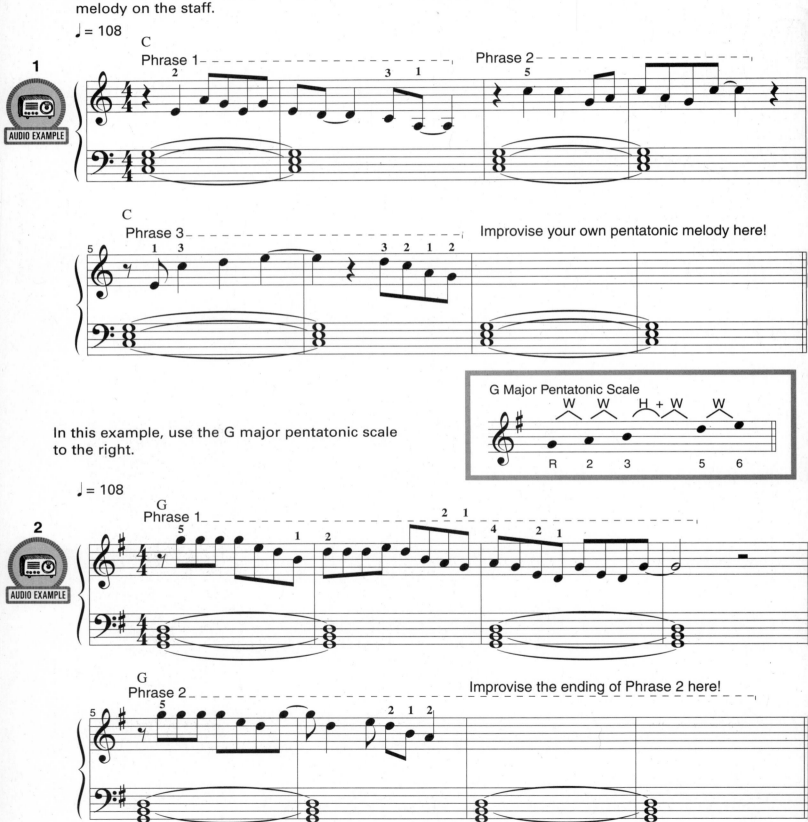

In this example, use the G major pentatonic scale to the right.

In this example, we use a different pentatonic scale for each chord. When the left hand plays a G chord, we play notes from the G major pentatonic scale. Over the C chord, we play the C major pentatonic. The chords to a song are often called *the changes*. Changing scales as the chords change is called *playing the change*s.

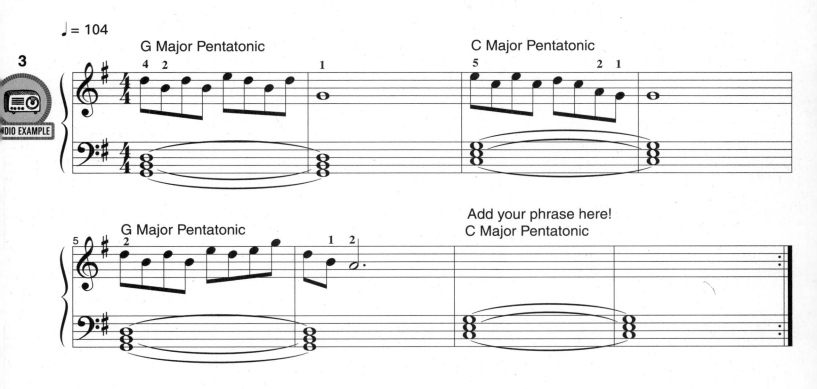

Chuck Leavell is an excellent keyboardist who made his reputation with the Allman Brothers Band. Since the 1970s, he has played with Eric Clapton, the Black Crowes and the Rolling Stones.

PHOTO • GENE SHAW/COURTESY OF STARFILES, INC.

Let's play the changes some more, but in the key of F with two new pentatonic scales: F and B♭. You're on your own—no tune has been provided. Improvise with gusto!

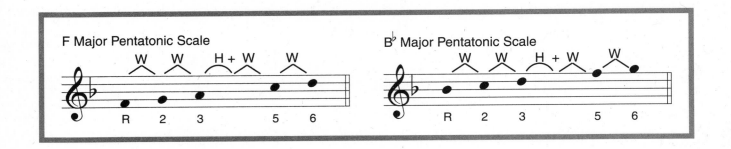

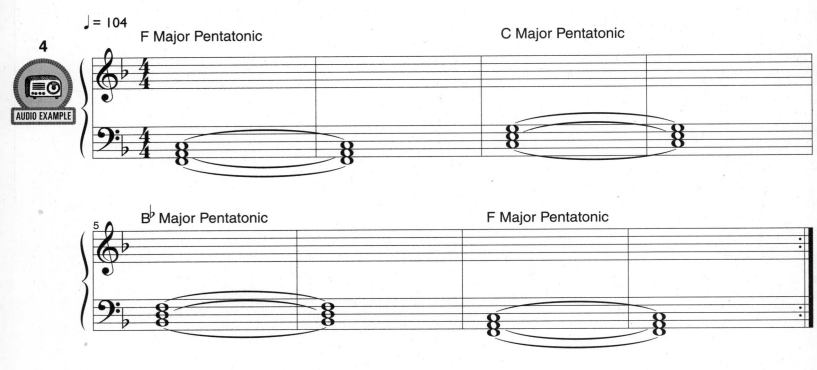

You can also play the major pentatonic scale of the key of the song all the way through, as we did on pages 131 and 132. After you play this example with the suggested scale on each chord, try playing just the F major pentatonic scale throughout. Listen to how well the notes fit, even as the chords change. This is because all of the chords are *diatonic* to the key of F major, which means they all belong to the key (they are the primary chords, see page 69), as are the notes of the scale. This is called *diatonic improvisation*.

In *Far As You Like*, try to determine where the pentatonic scales are changing with the chords. In the repeat of the A section, improvise your own melody in the right hand using these scales:

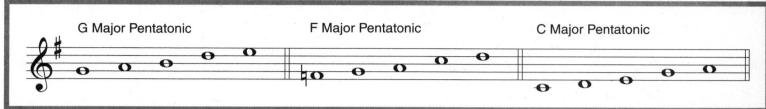

G Major Pentatonic   F Major Pentatonic   C Major Pentatonic

Far As You Like

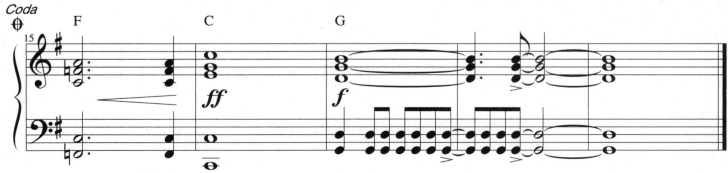

The Minor Pentatonic Scale

The minor pentatonic and major pentatonic scales are closely related but they sound very different. The major pentatonic scale has a country-music flavor but the minor pentatonic scale has a darker, bluesier sound. They are similar in that they both have five notes but they compare differently to the major scale.

Here is a C major scale and a C minor pentatonic scale. Notice that the 3rd and 7th of the minor pentatonic scale are flatted (♭3 and ♭7).

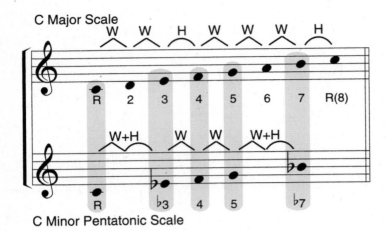

C Major Scale

C Minor Pentatonic Scale

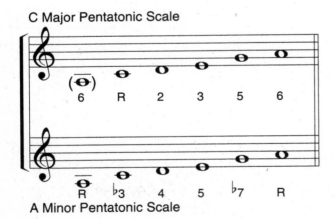

C Major Pentatonic Scale

A Minor Pentatonic Scale

To get a feeling for the minor pentatonic scale, learn to play "New Life." Notice the key signature. This tune is in the key of C minor.

New Life

♩ = 112

Billy Joel became a recording artist for Columbia Records in the 1970s. He is one of the most popular pianists in the world. His tour with superstar/pianist Elton John was a piano aficionado's dream.

Off the Main Highway uses the E minor pentatonic scale for the main melody. Notice that, except for the first two measures and the last, the song is repeated three times. Improvise your own melody over the repeats using the E minor pentatonic scale. Remember, you do not have to stay in the same octave as you improvise. Feel free to move the E minor pentatonic scale to different octaves.

Have fun!

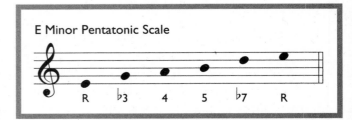

Off the Main Highway

THE BLUES

Blues music is at the heart of lots of great rock'n'roll. In fact, one could argue that if the blues didn't exist, rock'n'roll would never have developed. Rock music grew out of rhythm and blues in the 1950s, so, much of what we hear as rock music is really blues with a different beat.

The Blues Scale and Blue Notes

The major and minor pentatonic scales you learned in the last chapter are great tools for blues improvisation, and so is the *blues scale*. Below, the C blues scale is compared with the C major scale. The C blues scale is very similar to the C minor pentatonic scale except that it includes an additional flat 5 (♭5). The ♭5 is a very distinctive sound. It adds such an important twist to the blues sound that it is often called a *blue note*. Sometimes, for reasons of convenience, the ♭5 is written as a ♯4, its enharmonic equivalent.

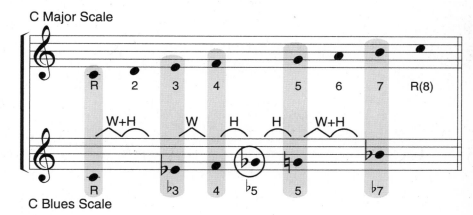

Here is a typical blues melody using the ♭5:

♩ = 96

Since blues harmony is more open to experimentation than many other musical styles, the blues performer has much more leeway in choosing notes for a solo. Quite often, the blues will freely combine major and minor sounds (major 3rds and minor 3rds) in a piece of music. The left hand might play harmony based on major chords while the right hand, or the soloist, plays a melody that is based on the minor chord! The minor 3rd (♭3) played against a major chord is another very important blue note.

Here is a short blues passage in G that typifies this combination of major (in the left hand) and minor (in the right hand).

The Blues in G

♩ = 92

See The Light demonstrates the use of the ♭5 in the key of E minor.

See the Light

The Grace Note

The *grace note* is like the spice in Louisiana cooking—a tiny bit goes a long way. Grace notes are little notes that precede a larger note called the *main note*. The two notes are usually connected with a small slur marking. To play a grace note, rob a bit of time from the main note and quickly play it before the main note. Some blues players actually slide their finger off the grace note on to the main note, especially if the grace note falls on a black key. Fingerings such as this are marked with a dash; 3-3 indicates to slide the 3rd finger from one key to the next.

To prepare for grace notes, play the exercise below. Notice that the ♭5 blue note is sometimes written as A♯ (if it is ascending) and sometimes as B♭ (if it is descending).

This time, three of the blue notes are shortened to become grace notes. In each case, quickly slide your finger off the black key to the white key. Don't worry about being rhythmically precise with the grace notes. There is some rhythmic freedom allowed in this style. The main thing is to have fun and "get the blues."

The Blues Shuffle or Swing Eighths

So far, all the eighth notes you have played have been *straight eighths*. That is, all the eighths were played evenly. The beats were evenly divided in two. There is another style of eighth notes called *swing eighths*. Swing eighths divide the beats into uneven eighth notes—the first eighth is held for about double the value of the second. We would say that music played with swing eighths is in *swing feel* or *shuffle feel*. Jazz musicians almost always play in swing feel, imitating the era of the great big band swing era. Early rock performers borrowed this feel, usually calling it a shuffle. It is an infectious beat and easy to feel, but there are special conventions for reading and writing them that you must learn.

Let's start by looking at a measure of straight eighths and a measure of eighth-note triplets.

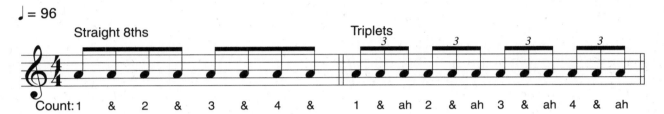

The next example shows swing eighths. In the first measure, the first two notes of each triplet are tied together. Count aloud "1-&-ah, 2-&-ah," etc. Clap on the numbers and the "ah's." In the second measure, the eighth notes look like straight eighths, but are counted and performed as swing eighths. Count and clap again. It should sound exactly like the first measure. That's right! Swing eighths look just like straight eighths. The important difference is the "Swing 8ths" mark above the music.

Sometimes the marking above the music will say "Swing Feel," or "Shuffle." In jazz music, those terms are often left out because the player assumes the music is in typical jazz swing feel. The reason for this predicament is that writing all the music in triplets would clutter up the page with little "3s." It's just tidier to do it this way.

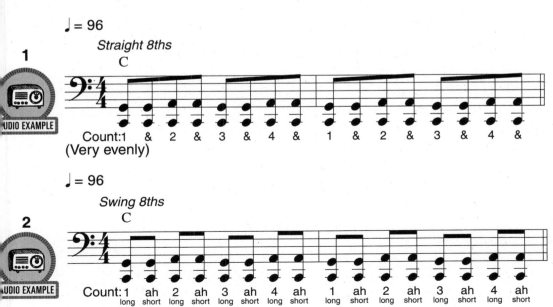

Let's play an old time rockin' shuffle in D. Practice each hand separately. Play very slowly at first to make sure both hands are coordinated. Keep a steady, driving beat throughout.

Roadhouse Deluxe

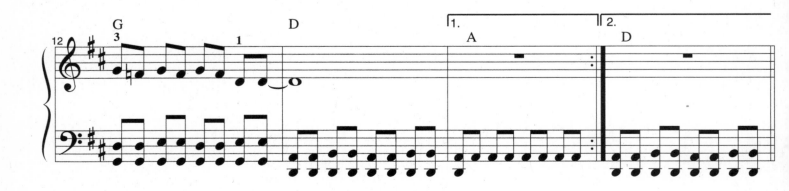

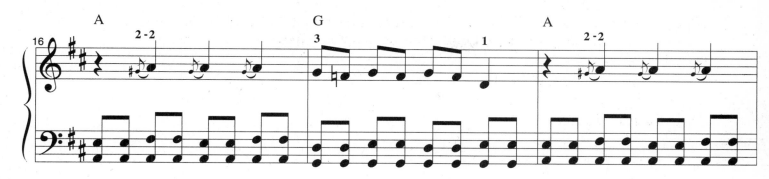

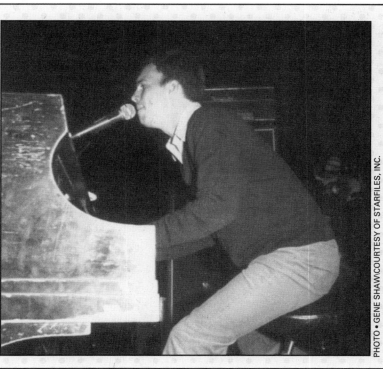

Ben Folds of Ben Folds Five is one of the hottest young pianists in contemporary music. With their hit CD, "Whatever and Ever Amen," released in 1997, they became well known throughout the music world. Ben Folds now has a successful solo career and is an accomplished player capable of everything from tender ballads to hard rocking pseudo-punk.

Here is a tune with a boogie bass line in the left hand. Concentrate on keeping the left hand steady as you play the melody in the right hand. If you play this with the proper attitude (rockin'!), your hands may get tired. If so, rest your hands a bit and play again with even *more* spirit! Seriously, you should be careful to avoid an overuse injury.

Honky Tonk Town

Here is a honky-tonk shuffle. Feel free to embellish the right hand with grace notes. That's right! Put 'em in wherever the spirit moves you.

No Easy Riders

♩ = 112

*Last time only.

The 12-Bar Blues

Most blues songs, and most blues-based rock songs, have a structure we call the *12-bar blues*. Obviously, the form is twelve bars long! The form can be repeated as many times as you like. Each time through the 12-bar form is called a *chorus*.

Using Roman numerals to identify the chords, here is the formula for a basic 12-bar blues:

4	measures of	I
2	measures of	IV
2	measures of	I
1	measure of	V
1	measure of	IV
2	measures of	I
12	**measures**	**of blues!**

This chord pattern is the universal language of the blues, and all rock players should know it in all key signatures. Here is a 12-bar blues in G:

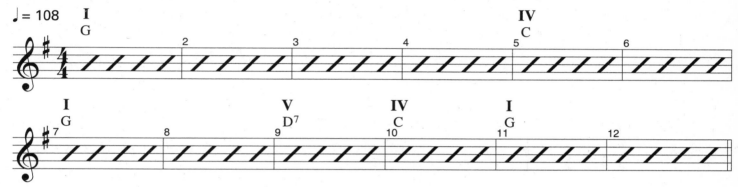

For practice, play this blues with simple triads.

IVE IT A TRY

Transposing

Using the Roman numerals, it is possible to move this chord progression to any key. This is called *transposing*. You can start on any triad and apply this formula, and you'll be playing the blues. Every day, try playing this pattern in another key. Follow the circle of 5ths (see page 224) order. A seasoned player will know the blues in any key.

The following chart will help you play the blues in any key:

Primary Chords in All Twelve Keys

Major Key	I	IV	V
C	C	F	G
G	G	C	D
D	D	G	A
A	A	D	E
E	E	A	B
B	B	E	F♯
G♭	G♭	C♭	D♭
D♭	D♭	G♭	A♭
A♭	A♭	D♭	E♭
E♭	E♭	A♭	B♭
B♭	B♭	E♭	F
F	F	B♭	C

This song uses straight blues changes with a moving bass line in the first chorus. In this chorus, you are accompanying (*comping*). Notice the slash chords that appear at the ends of the measures. Between bars 22 and 24 the chords are not from the standard blues progression and instead, the chords follow the circle of fifths (page 224) which adds variety to the progression. The E7 and A7 chords are not in the standard G blues progression but they both lead to D7 when moving around the circle. Enjoy the sound!

Take to the Road

2nd Chorus Solo

Blues Line in the Bass = Rock Power Riffs

When blues riffs are used in the left hand, they can be the basis of some very hot bass lines.

Play a C7 chord in the right hand and try the left-hand line in this example.

 To get even more power out of a blues riff, double the notes with the right hand one octave higher. Notice that in the next example both hands are playing in bass clef.

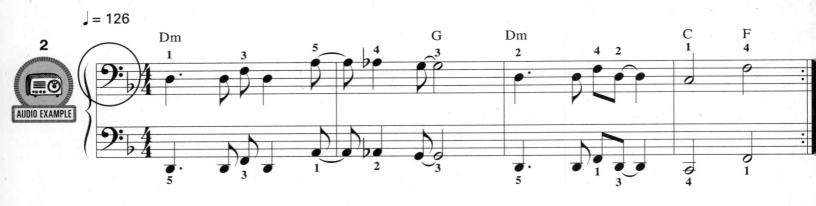

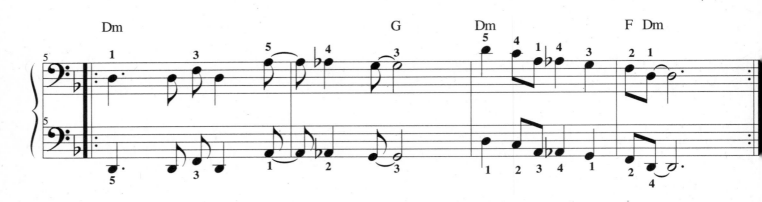

Try doubling this bass line with your right hand.

In the A section of the next example, double the bass line with your right hand. In the B section, play the triads indicated above the staff. In bars 8 and 12, go back to doubling the bass line with your right hand.

FUNKY SIXTEENTHS

Most early rock was based around straight- or swing-eighth notes. They are usually easy to play, read and understand. This section deals with sixteenth-note rhythms.

In the late 1960s and into the 1970s, pop music became more rhythmically complex.

Sixteenth-note rhythms became more common. Listeners and dancers, in particular, really liked what sixteenths did to the beat. It added "the FUNK." The soul music explosion of the late 1960s (Motown) moved this style to the forefront of rock and pop music. Rock players were looking for new ways of making *the groove* happen.

Here is a typical bass part using only eighth notes:

♩ = 104

It is a perfectly good bass line. It has a strong root feel and moves things along. But suppose it's the last set of the night, the bass player gets a little punchy and holds the first note of the line just one quarter beat too long. This is what happens:

♩ = 104

All of a sudden the bass line starts getting a little loose! The drummer senses what's going on and starts hitting a fat back beat (strong accents on the 2nd and 4th beats). People start dancing like crazy and a new style of music is born!

Sixteenth notes look more formidable than they are. All you have to do is divide the beat into four parts instead of two. They are twice as fast as eighth notes. The next example compares eighth notes and sixteenths. For the sixteenth notes, count "1-e-&-ah, 2-e-&-ah, 3-e-&-ah, 4-e-&-ah."

♩ = 80

8th Notes (Two per beat)   16th Notes (Four per beat)

1   &   2   &   3   &   4   &   1 e & ah 2 e & ah 3 e & ah 4 e & ah

At first, play sixteenth-note passages slowly to ensure accuracy.

To play repeating sixteenths at a faster tempo, some special techniques can be utilized. The next example shows a way of alternating fingers, right and left, to play rapidly. This method is especially great if you need a rapid, machine-gun-style riff.

♩ = 96

1 e & ah 2 e & ah 3 e & ah 4 e & ah   1 e & ah 2 e & ah 3 e & ah 4 e & ah

Such rapid passages are unusual in rock songs. They are sometimes novelty parts, or a bit of flash to see how quickly the keyboardist can play. More practical are syncopated parts where the keyboardist breaks up the pattern with off-beat accents to make a tune really groove.

Below is a bass line written in two different ways. First, it is written over two measures in eighth notes, then in one measure with sixteenth notes. The two versions will sound identical but in the second version, the beats move twice as slow. This is called *half time.* It takes up half the space and is the way funk lines are usually written.

Here is a variation on the bass line from example 94 with variations in the right hand part. Notice the intensive use of syncopation. Syncopation with sixteenths is what funk rhythms are all about.

Explosive Soul

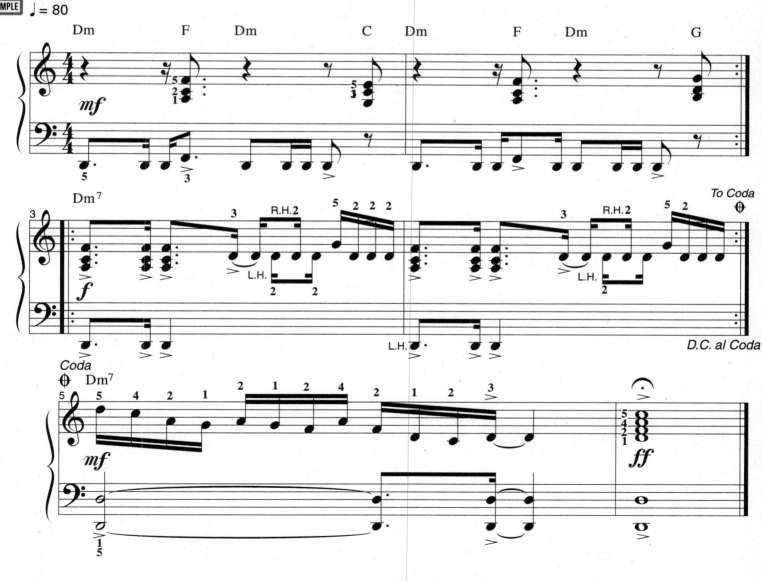

PART 3: BEING A PROFESSIONAL KEYBOARDIST

Playing keyboards in a band is fun and rewarding. Having acquired the skills and knowledge offered in this book so far, you are probably ready to play in a band. This section of the book provides tips on starting or joining a band, preparing for an audition, rehearsing and gigging. Finally, you'll gain some insights into the music business, discover how to protect your interests and eventually get a recording contract. Let's get started.

CHOOSING YOUR EQUIPMENT

A major aspect of being a modern-day keyboardist is—surprise!—owning keyboards. There is a constant struggle to keep your equipment up-to-date and your sounds current. Technology is constantly changing, and many keyboardists want to have all of the latest gear. While major revolutions in synthesizer technology are not happening now as quickly as they did in years past, there will always be some new product that seems better than what you already have.

Keyboard players have it rough. Other musicians expect us to know everything and to always have the proper sound for a particular musical moment. Guitarists have six strings, but keyboardists have as many as 88 keys. All of those buttons to push and sounds to know—what is a keyboard player to do?

The first thing to do is to figure out exactly what gear you need in order to perform your music the way you want. If money is a factor, you will also need to figure out the cheapest way to do it all without sacrificing too much.

Keyboards

Different musical styles call for different keyboard setups. A jazz piano player will probably not need a $5,000 synthesizer, and a Top-40 keyboardist will probably be unhappy with just a digital piano. Here are several different types of keyboard to consider:

Pianos

The piano has been around for over 200 years but hasn't really become any more portable in that time. However, recent developments in the digital piano realm have made it cheaper and easier to have an instrument that both sounds and feels good. A digital piano usually consists of 73 to 88 weighted keys with a variety of sampled piano sounds from which to choose. These pianos can weigh anywhere from 40 pounds on up, and cost anywhere from $800 to over $3,000. Some have features you may not need, so a careful look into what each model offers is recommended—especially if you're shopping on a limited budget. In general, look for an instrument with a good piano sound and feel, MIDI ports (both in and out) and a weight you could tote a few blocks if you really had to (e.g., if your car breaks down or you must rely on public transportation).

Electric Pianos

Although samplers and digital pianos have largely displaced them, there are still many keyboardists lugging around dinosaur keyboards from the 1970s. The two most popular electric pianos from that era are the Fender Rhodes and the Wurlitzer. Each has an instantly recognizable sound that many keyboardists find impossible to duplicate with a sampler. Depending on your needs, one of these models might be good for your live rig, but only if you find that it defines your sound. Less picky players will find most synthesized or sampled electric pianos sufficient. They're also a lot easier to carry around than a Rhodes.

Synthesizers

The term "synthesizer" (often shortened to "synth") applies to any keyboard that creates its sounds electronically through the use of oscillators, filters and all sorts of other things most of us never fully understand. Suffice it to say that synths can create a wide variety of sounds, both electronic and acoustic in character. There are many different types of synths, with a main distinction being *digital* or *analog.* The synths of the 1970s and early 1980s were primarily analog. When Yamaha introduced the DX-7 in 1983, it was the first affordable digital synth. Today, most synths are digital in some respect, but the warmer sound of an analog synth can be emulated with digital technology. Some synths, known as *workstations,* are all-in-one machines. They combine multitimbral capabilities (meaning that more than one type of sound can be played at a time) with an on-board *sequencer,* a device that enables you to create entire songs with drums and other instruments through just one unit. This is great if you want to do some sequencing for a live gig, or if you just can't afford a computer-based sequencer.

Organs

The granddaddy of all electric organs is the Hammond B-3, usually amplified by a Leslie rotating speaker. The sound of this combination is legendary, but moving either piece of equipment is only slightly easier than moving a house down the street. Most synths have decent organ sounds that will satisfy all but the die-hard organist. There are also a number of portable organs on the market that emulate the B-3 with its drawbars and settings. Other organs that have achieved a certain notoriety are the Vox and the Farfisa. Both of these have a different sound than the B-3; both sound cheesy to some people, amazing to others. They were most popular in the 1960s as cheaper and lighter alternatives to the B-3.

Other Keyboards

There are many other kinds of keyboards out there that you can use in interesting and creative ways: the Clavinet, the mellotron and its cousin the Chamberlain, the melodica and, of course, Uncle Murray's favorite, the accordion, which is enjoying a renaissance. One easy way to get to know the sounds of all of these instruments is to find patches on synths that recreate them.

Samplers

A sampler is really just a digital tape recorder. It copies the sound of something played into it and stores it so it can be played via a keyboard. Samples can be used in many ways, either each individually as a copy of an existing instrument's sound (like the aforementioned Fender Rhodes sample) or together, with several different sounds combined into one. For instance, you could combine a sampled string sound with a more synth-like patch to create an interesting layer for a song.

Modules

A sound module is really just a synth or sampler with no keyboard. A module is considerably smaller and cheaper than a synth with keys. A MIDI cable connects a module to a master keyboard, which then controls the sound coming from the module. A drawback to having a module is that a lot of the buttons and controls are hidden within other buttons and controls to save space. Some people don't like using them in a live rig, as you can't always see or control the knobs while playing the master keyboard. But for building up a MIDI studio, modules are indispensable; more about them later.

Amplification

There are many ways to amplify your keyboards. Keyboard amps have become popular and more compact, and they are good at capturing much of a keyboard's dynamic range. You can also get a small PA system to create a little more clarity in your sound. A keyboard amp is a good first amp, but make sure you like the sound before you buy one. Also, pick it up to feel its weight—remember that you'll have to carry it! Check the power rating to make sure it can put out enough juice for your situation. Keyboard amps require more power than guitar amps, so a 60-watt keyboard amp won't sound as loud as a 60-watt guitar amp. The differences between the two types of amps are that the keyboard model will provide a cleaner sound and can handle lower and higher frequencies better than the guitar amp.

Stands and Setups

After a while, using an old card table as a keyboard stand just isn't a good idea. There are many types of stands made especially for keyboards, and they come in different styles and, of course, prices. If you plan on having one keyboard, a single-tiered stand should be fine. Some keyboardists prefer to play standing up, while some prefer the traditional sitting-down approach. Use whichever method works for you.

If you have a two-tiered stand or more than two keyboards, make sure that each keyboard is at a comfortable playing level. A keyboard placed too high or too low will make it difficult to play and may cause tension in the arms, neck and shoulders. You should be able to see all of the readouts of your keyboards without craning your neck or straining your eyes. If you have more than two keyboards, make the keyboards on the lower level even in height—this will make it easier to switch from one to another.

When you set up, you'll want your amplifier or speaker to be as close to you as possible without it being right on top of you. Place it either behind you or slightly off to the side. This will make it easier for you to hear and allow you easy access to controls and knobs during a gig. It's often a good idea to elevate the amplifier somewhat so that it is closer to your ears and so that the sound projects to you and the crowd rather than straight into your legs or back.

Here is a typical and generally effective layout for your gig setup:

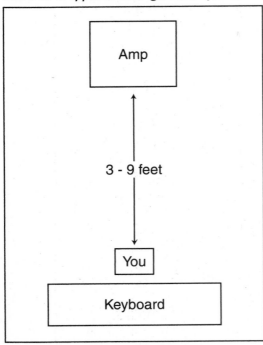

Your First Rig

If you're getting a rig together for the first time, you'll probably want to base your setup around one keyboard, most likely a synthesizer of some sort. Chances are you probably already have at least one keyboard. If not, here are some ideas for what to look for in an instrument.

1. **A wide variety of good sounds**. A modern-day synth should be able to emulate a number of acoustic instruments, such as pianos, strings, organs, drums, etc. Some synths focus on creating purely synthesized sounds, which is great if that is what you need. But if you want something that can emulate other instruments or even other synthesizers (e.g., Moogs, Oberheims, etc.), then you will probably need a keyboard that replicates these sounds fairly well.

2. **An action that feels right to you**. If you have grown up playing piano your whole life, a light keyboard action might not appeal to you. Take some time to play a particular keyboard at a music store before you buy it. Hearing a demo or reading a great review will not allow you to judge whether or not a particular keyboard is right for you.

3. **Multitimbral capability**. Multitimbral synths can play more than one kind of sound at once if you use the "multi" mode with a sequencer. If you plan on using a synth only as a live keyboard, this feature is generally not a necessity; for studio work, however, it is a must.

4. **Touch sensitivity**. Most keyboards now have touch sensitivity, which means that the harder you strike a key, the louder the sound that is produced. Not all sounds in a keyboard have this programmed into them, and not all need it. Classic analog synth sounds have a history of lacking touch sensitivity (touch sensitivity wasn't widely available until the early 1980s), so newer synth sounds modeled after the classic synths will often have the touch sensitivity disabled. Touch sensitivity is most useful in patches like piano or electric piano sounds, or acoustic simulations in which different degrees of dynamics and attacks are needed.

5. **A fit with your budget.** The first synth you buy doesn't need to be the be-all-and-end-all keyboard of your rig. Besides, keyboard technology changes so quickly that today's hot synth will sound mediocre in a few years. Find one keyboard that fits most, if not all, of your needs, and get to know it inside and out. Read the manual carefully and *really learn* how to work with the existing sounds and create new ones. Many keyboardists and producers started out with a small amount of gear and have gotten to know their equipment so well that their music sounds like it came from a rig five times the size and price. Shop around—compare different prices and keyboards. Don't believe every salesperson you speak to; for one reason or another, he or she may be pressuring you to buy something you don't need.

USING YOUR KEYBOARD'S SOUNDS

You might have noticed in your keyboard manual that you are told what a sound is like, but not how you could or should use it. That's because creativity cannot necessarily be taught. Perhaps the manual wasn't written by a creative musician. So, how do you use the sounds you have at your disposal in your synthesizer?

Most modern synthesizers have a broad spectrum of sounds to choose from. Many keyboards come with hundreds of built-in sounds, plus room to create and program your own. It can all be overwhelming, but don't despair quite yet. Let's first look at a few basic varieties of sounds.

Keyboard Instrument Sounds
Acoustic Piano Sounds

Keyboard sounds, not surprisingly, emulate different types of keyboard instruments. Generally, the most important sound is that of the granddaddy of all keyboards, the piano. Keyboard-produced piano sounds, whether sampled or synthesized, will most likely allow for touch sensitivity, a full dynamic range and a clear sound. Hopefully, they will also sound like pianos. Piano sounds can be straight or contain a "pad" (an additional layer). Straight piano sounds will be designated by descriptions like "bright," "warm" or "medium" layered sounds will have names like "Piano Pad," "Piano/Strings," "Piano Layer" and so on. The *timbral* (characteristics of tone) differences among these can be drastic. For live gigs and louder musical environments, a bright piano setting (one with an abundance of high frequencies) can work well. Layered timbres work best in situations requiring a smooth harmonic sound coupled with a strong, moving melodic voice. These sounds are ideal for pop ballads and other songs in which the keyboard plays an important role.

You can do many things with a piano sound; it is probably the most versatile keyboard sound you have. The percussive attack allows the sound to cut through even the heaviest of accompaniments, while the mellow ring from the piano strings provides that sustained sound that is so familiar. When a sound like this contains a wide range of dynamics and attacks, the different colors you can achieve are seemingly innumerable.

Example 1 shows the piano's ability to establish the harmony while providing a rhythmic foundation. Example 2 lays out the chords with no movement between them. You could think of these examples as repetitions of the same section. Example 2 could be used in Verse 1 of a song, and Example 1 could be used in Verse 2. The simple chording of Example 2 would probably work best in an early section of a song, as it is simpler and allows for a piece to build. The rhythmic nature of Example 1 might be better suited to a later section of a song, (i.e., after it has built itself up dynamically). By subtly varying your piano arrangement from section to section, you can create a piece of music that is not only more interesting, but also builds as it goes along and contains more dynamic contrasts and a more interesting contour.

In softer music, like a ballad, the piano can be either the focal point or the accompaniment...

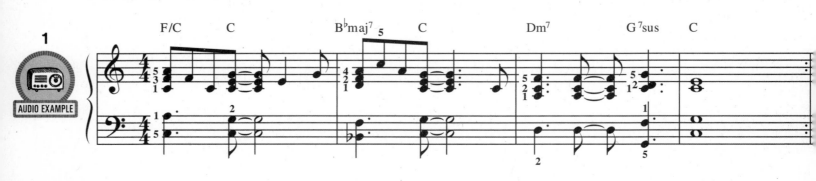

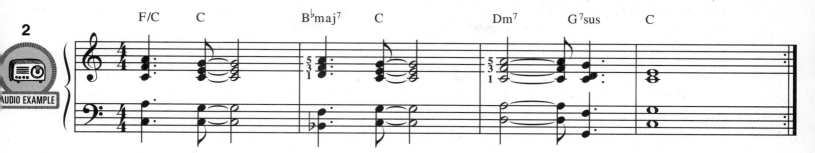

For mid-tempo songs, you can use the piano in many different ways, whether to lay out the chords in a simple fashion (Example 3A), add some small accents (Example 3B) or play a static eighth-note figure (Example 3C).

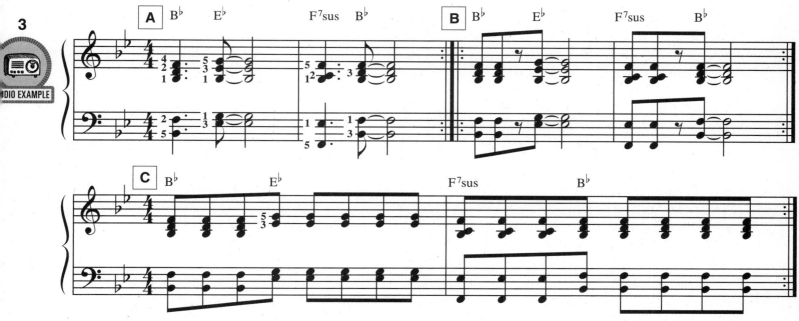

The beauty and transparency of the piano becomes most apparent in the upper register, which starts roughly two octaves above middle C. The bell-like tones of these notes can be very effective in certain passages, such as the rolling arpeggio in Example 4A and the static rhythms of Examples 4B and 4C.

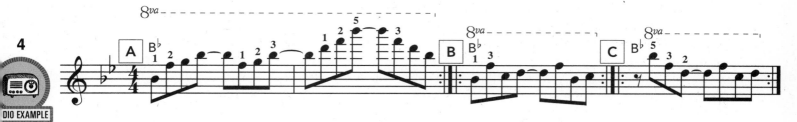

These ideas will not overpower other instruments, but will instead stand out in an arrangement. Use them with discretion, however. Overkill can be a factor when a certain range is used too often.

You can also double a bass line, either in part or in full, to thicken up a sound. Another idea is to play the root of a chord strongly. This works best at the beginning of a section or phrase, and works even better when the harmony preceding it is slightly different and the harmony following it doesn't change for several bars. In other words, it's best to let the notes ring for maximum effect:

Electric Piano Sounds

Electric piano sounds are labeled with names like "E. Piano," "Rhodes," "Wurlitzer" and so forth. A more trebly sound will have the word "tine" in it (tines are the tone bars used in most electric pianos). A tine-like sound is crisper, as opposed to the warmer sound of, say, 1970s electric pianos. The term "FM Piano" refers to an even brighter electric piano sound; the Yamaha DX-7, which uses digital FM (frequency modulation), spawned a slew of electric piano sounds in the 1980s. These sounds are easily recognizable and work well as an addition to a pad or string sound.

In a situation that requires a strong sound, a percussive attack works best. Try these examples using a sound with a percussive attack.

The two electric piano sounds that are most often reproduced are the Rhodes and the Wurlitzer. The Rhodes sound is generally recognizably thick. The Wurlitzer has a strong attack and a thinner sound, enabling it to blend into a track more easily.

A percussive attack can still be used in electric piano sounds in a less "active" section of a song, as long as the sound has some sustaining power. The attack cuts through the instrument mix, while the sustaining power of the sound carries the harmony. These patterns are good for these purposes and can be used in many different situations.

| — = Tenuto |
| (sustained) |

A warm electric piano sound works well for pop and R&B ballads. It can be the focal point of the arrangement...

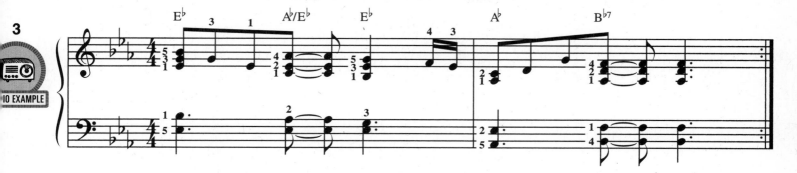

...or fulfill a supporting role alongside a guitar or other sustaining sound.

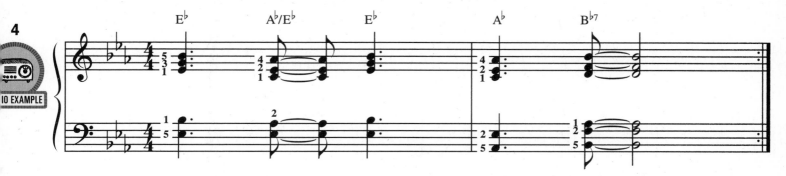

Notice how the first example above is busier and more rhythmic. As you play the second example, imagine a string pad or similar sound behind your part.

Organ Sounds

Organ sounds vary widely, from Hammond B-3 emulations to the church pipe organ sound we all know and fear. Some Hammond emulations will be smooth and clean, ideal for slower or mellower music, and some will have built-in distortion that begs you to play it as loudly and obnoxiously as possible.

Organ sounds tend to have similar shapes—that is, they always have an immediate attack when you depress a key and an immediate release when you let go of it. They also sustain indefinitely as long as you keep a key depressed. Otherwise, the sonic possibilities of organ sounds are endless.

You can use a mellower organ sound for slower ballads. These sounds should not be too heavy, distorted or overpowering. Using the basic elements of voice leading, you should be able to create a part that seems like it never moves, even though it does.

A slightly more percussive sound can be used in a more rhythmic setting. Play these examples with a percussive organ patch, accenting the staccato nature of each phrase.

The most powerful organ is one with a downright nasty and distorted sound. If you have a screamingly loud and ugly organ sound in your keyboard, try this: play a glissando up to the highest note and hold it. If it's a well-programmed and/or well-sampled sound, you will feel the power of the real B-3. The real thing seems to weigh as much as a cow, so the advantage of a good substitute is clear.

Play this example, holding the high B with your fifth finger while playing the lower notes with your left hand.

For a more rhythmic and upfront approach, try the following variation.

Harpsichords, Clavinets ("Clavs") and Mellotrons

Harpsichords, Clavinets and mellotrons are all real keyboard instruments that synthesizers emulate. A harpsichord has strings much like a piano; unlike a piano, though, the strings are plucked by quills instead of struck by hammers, resulting in a more staccato sound. A Clavinet is basically an amplified harpsichord. The mellotron is a keyboard from the 1970s that uses analog tape loops containing samples of different acoustic instruments. It has a recognizable sound often emulated in synthesizers.

Other Instrument Sounds

Synthesizers also emulate a wide variety of other instruments, with mixed results. It's difficult to capture and/or replicate all of the subtleties of all acoustic instruments. Some wind instruments, like trumpets and saxophones, are hard to duplicate with synths and samplers. Other instruments, such as strings, percussion and some woodwinds, can be imitated fairly well. If you want to use a sound modeled on an actual instrument, it's helpful to learn about the instrument—its range, the way in which it is played, and so on. This will make your use of the sound less artificial, and this information is useful to know even if you don't necessarily want the patch to sound like the instrument. Drum sounds, in particular, sound better if they are played with some idea of how real drums are played.

Using Pads

Pads are smooth, string-like sounds that can fill out the harmony of a song. They work especially well in slower tempos or in sections where other instruments are more percussive; they can smooth out the sound of the song as a whole. Some pads have a "violin-ish" sound to them, while others sound more electronic or synthesized. Labels such as "Strings" and "String Pad" denote a more acoustic string pad sound. Other pad sounds can vary widely in sound and timbre. Some will have a slow attack, meaning that the sound is not heard immediately after striking a key. These slower-moving sounds work best in songs or sections with slower tempos or those that don't require sharp attacks. Other sounds will have a long decay or release, meaning that the notes will linger after you let go of them. Each pad sound has its own characteristics which can be understood only by listening to it and judging whether it works well in a particular musical situation.

Play through each of your synth's sounds. Keep an ear out for pad sounds that you like and think will be useful. Write down the name and location, as well as a brief description (big, warm, transparent, etc.) of each. When you have this information in front of you, you'll be able to move from sound to sound quickly, which is helpful when you either are unfamiliar with a piece of music or wish to use many different sounds within a song. For example, you may wish to use a thinner sound for the first verse of a song and then bigger or broader sounds for the following sections as the song builds in intensity and dynamic level.

In addition to changing sounds, you can also vary your voicings, making them denser for louder sections and sparser for softer sections. This is a more "organic" way to control dynamic levels without having to resort to the volume controls.

Use the chord progression at the top of page 164 to practice changing your pad sounds. Use a softer and more transparent sound for the first two verses, and then change to thicker and heavier sounds as the song progresses and grows in dynamic level and intensity. Try not to use sounds that are *too* different from each other, as you should ideally create smooth transitions between sections. Use a bigger sound for the second chorus than you do for the first.

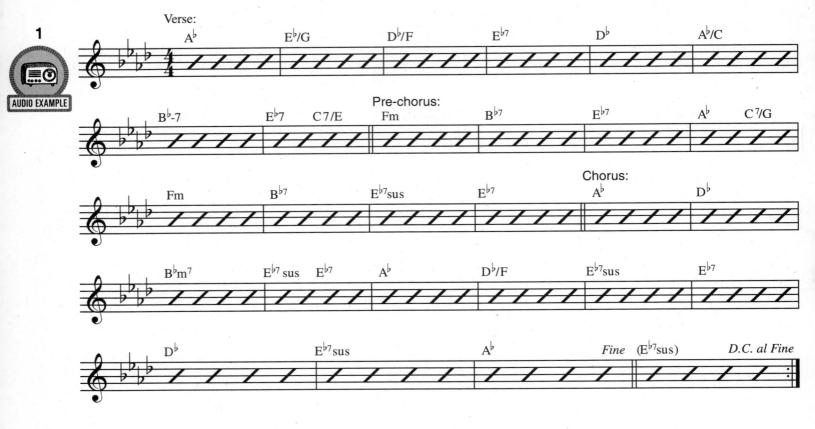

Here are some ideas to use to create natural dynamics with your voicings. For softer sections of a song, a voicing of only two notes will work quite well. Add notes as the song progresses, and vary the spacing between the notes.

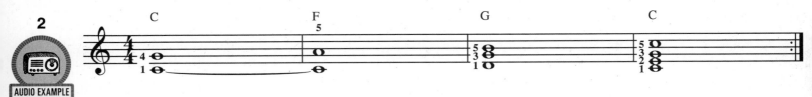

Try spreading your voicings over more than an octave using simple voice leading. This will give the impression of space while still defining the tonality.

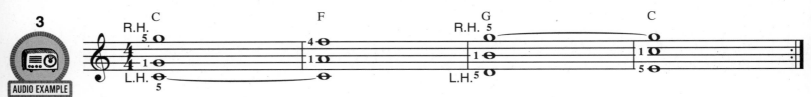

A simple triad will work well for louder sections of a tune, especially if you add the root and 5th to the bottom of the voicing.

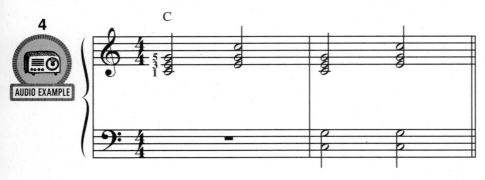

Synthesized Sounds

You've already used some synthesizer sounds in your pads, but there are many different synthed sounds that modern synthesizers can produce. This is really where the instrument gets a chance to shine. Some sounds are warm, others crisp, but they all have an electronic feel. The range of textures is tremendous, from mild pad-like colors to unearthly sonic shapes. Special effects and noises also fall into the category of synthed sounds; they have seemingly unlimited sonic possibilities. Some sounds are labeled with names like "Synth Piano," "Synth Organ" or "Synth Pad." These names can mean that the sounds on which they are based are further modified by other electronic sounds. Again, exploring the different sounds and what they can do is the only way to really learn about them and determine how and where to use them.

Synthesizers have come a long way since the first Moog synths appeared in the 1960s. It took time for them to gain acceptance by musicians and listeners, but by the mid-1970s, synths could be found in many recordings. Now they are everywhere, in everything from mellow new-age music to hard-hitting techno. They play drum sounds and orchestra sounds, as well as many "invented" sounds you may have never heard before.

Different Types of Synthesized Sounds

There are too many types of synth sounds to cover all of them within the scope of this book, but here are a few basic categories as well as ways in which they can be used.

Analog-style synth sounds cover a wide sonic spectrum, but they have some common elements. These patches have a warmer (as opposed to a more metallic) sound, an immediate attack and a slight brassiness. They are best for powerful chording and some lead lines. Try these ideas with several different analog-style sounds.

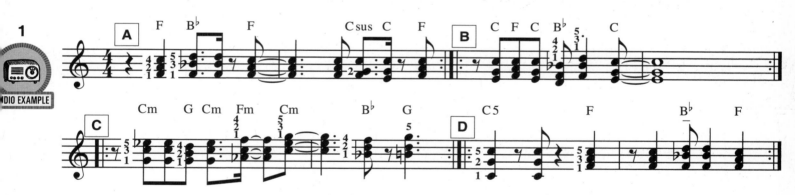

Some patches are more percussive, somewhat like the sounds produced by a guitar or Clavinet. These are ideal for syncopated comping rhythms, especially when they are played staccato.

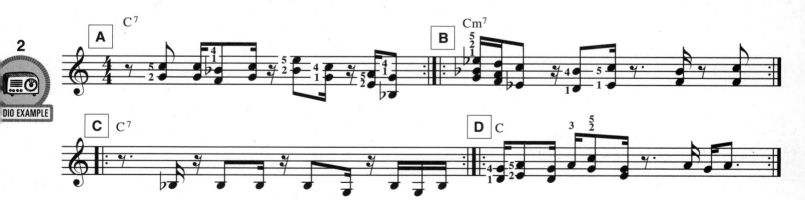

Special effects can be imitations of real sounds—like helicopters or nuclear explosions—or can be manufactured wholly from someone's imagination. Every synth has a few of these sounds; they can be fun to play with at first, but they have limited usefulness. If you do use a special-effect sound, it's best to do so sparingly.

A *sweep* sound is a cross between a pad and a special effect. The fundamental (root) tone will be present, but there will also be a filter sweep that attacks as the keys are held down. Some sweep sounds can make your synth sound like it is being sucked down the funnel of a tornado. Sweep sounds based on the root or a two- or three-note voicing work well at beginnings of phrases. Still, as with all special effects, they should be used with discretion.

3

A *lead* sound is a patch designed for solos or other melodic parts. Lead sounds are generally monophonic (i.e., only one note can be played at a time) and have an immediate attack. Some are big in sound, some subtle. When you use a lead sound, make sure that it works well with the mood of the song. A loud, cutting patch might not mesh well with a smooth ballad, and a dreamy lead sound probably won't cut through a louder, driving song.

Lead sounds are most effective when you use your keyboard's pitch-bending and modulating capabilities. Set your pitch-bend range to one whole step—this will make the pitch bend a whole step in either direction. You can think of the pitch bender as producing an effect similar to that of a guitarist bending a string (guitarists often bend their strings up a half or whole step to make the sound more expressive). Try this exercise, bending up on notes as indicated.

```
♩ = Bend up
```

4

When mastered, this technique can offer new levels of expression. In addition to pitch bending, you can also introduce *modulation* into the sound. When you add modulation through the use of either a mod wheel or a joystick, the distance between sound waves changes. The more modulation you add, the heavier the vibrato effect. Try this exercise using modulation at the points marked with an "X."

5

Listen to other synth players for soloing ideas, especially in the way of pitch-bending and modulation techniques. These techniques give you powers of expression much like you would have with an acoustic instrument, and can be very effective in making your solos sound more natural.

CREATING A MIDI SETUP

Setting up a studio of your own is a relatively easy and (mostly) affordable task. MIDI has made sequencing multiple keyboards and modules a practical way of creating your own music with top-quality sound. Creating music at home is now cheaper and easier than ever before. The setup requires a certain financial investment, but it can be well worth the price if you want to record your own music or hire yourself out to record and/or produce the music of others.

Wondrous new gadgets that make you green with gear envy seem to come out on a daily basis. However, if your budget is somewhat constrained (as most budgets are), you'll do well by sticking to the basic elements of a MIDI setup.

Basic Gear

There are a number of items of equipment necessary for a MIDI rig of any size. Most gear is available in a variety of brands and prices. A higher price usually indicates higher quality, but there are inexpensive models of just about everything that will work well for both beginning and advanced applications. Do your research before you buy a piece of gear—read reviews in magazines or on-line, or ask MIDI-savvy friends to recommend gear. You can also save money by buying used gear, but make certain it's working properly before you buy it.

Here are the elements of a basic MIDI setup:

1. **Something to record to**. This is essentially a means of storage for your music—a way to save it for playback. Analog multitrack recorders are good and can add a warmth that some people prefer, but they can be difficult to maintain, and the tapes can be expensive. Digital multitracks are very popular, as they can record eight tracks onto a digital tape and can be linked to each other to create 16, 24 or more tracks; most pro studios have some form of digital multitrack. They are somewhat portable as well, but also require a good deal of maintenance; Hard-disk recorders, both computer-based recorders that run in connection with your personal computer and stand-alone recorders that do essentially the same thing within a self-contained unit, are quickly becoming an inexpensive route to follow. Hard-disk recording can be more challenging to learn, but it allows you to do things that would be difficult to accomplish in traditional recording. You can, for instance, use software to copy or move one recorded track to another section of a tune, change the time, duration and pitch of a chosen note and so forth. There seems to be a new hard-disk medium coming out every six months or so, so do your research to figure out which system works best for you and your budget.

2. **Mixer**. Mixers are basically the traffic directors for all incoming and outgoing sound. All audio input (instruments, microphones and other sound sources such as CD, mp3 players and tape players), your recording device and (sometimes) your computer "meet" in the mixer. Each instrument is assigned its own channel, and multitimbral synths will have even more depending on the number of outputs. There are many kinds of mixers, some quite large and expensive, but for a beginning studio, you probably won't need more than a 16-channel mixer. If you plan on recording live instruments or vocals, you'll need a mixer that can accept microphone (i.e., analog) signals. If you plan on using only MIDI and keyboard (i.e., digital) sounds, you can get away with a simple line mixer that routes all the tracks to an overall mix. All mixers have controls for volume, equalization and effects that can be applied to each input (or "track"). The various tracks are fed into the master mix, which is then sent to the recording device.

3. **Monitors**. You might think that listening to everything on headphones seems like a good idea, but it is also helpful to be able to hear your music through a set of stereo monitors as it's recorded. Monitors can tell you what the mix will sound like in a room, while headphones are most useful for listening to details in a mix. You can buy powered monitors, which have power amps built into them to amplify the sound, or you can get unpowered monitors, which require the use of an external power amp. There are differences of opinion as to which type of system sounds best, and you should decide for yourself which you prefer. Listen for clarity in the high and low ends and make sure that the sound is consistent and even throughout the entire spectrum.

4. **Sequencer**. There are many different ways to sequence your music. Sequencing is basically a form of multitracking, with the sequencer controlling most parameters for each track. When you play a MIDI keyboard into a sequencer, the sequencer captures all the notes and MIDI information, allowing it to be played back exactly as you originally played it. Sequencers can also *quantize* tracks—that is, "round off" uneven or shorter rhythmic values to a larger preset value. Sequencers allow you to edit, create and save tracks without having to dump them to a recording medium right away. Stand-alone sequencers have a portability advantage, but most studios have some kind of computer-based sequencer, often combined with a hard-disk recorder, so that a sequence can be run and recorded to a hard disk simultaneously. This is quickly becoming the standard system, and it is getting cheaper and easier to own and operate.

5. **Keyboards**. A multitimbral synth of some sort will serve you well, as you can assign different patches to different MIDI channels, giving you more sonic capability. Modules can be a cheap and easy means of adding to your sound palette, and they don't take up nearly as much space as a keyboard. Use one dedicated keyboard as your controller, i.e., the instrument through which you input information to the sequencer. This controller should be touch and velocity sensitive, and have at least 61 keys.

6. **Something to mix down to**. You'll need a CD or DVD burner to save all your mixes to a portable medium. After you've completed the recording process, you'll record all of your mixes to one of these to create a master. Choose whichever offers the best features for your needs.

7. **Miscellaneous hardware**. You will also need things like keyboard stands, racks, cables, microphone stands, etc. in your studio setup. Racks are useful for keeping your workspace neat, which will make the recording process easier and more efficient. Make sure that any gear you install in a rack is solidly mounted. Good cables are a necessity; when purchasing cables, always buy at least one extra cable of each type.

Using Different Kinds of Pedals and Effects

A keyboard's sound can be manipulated through the use of effects, both built-in and external (sometimes called "outboard gear"). It is worthwhile to learn everything you can about the different types of effects built into your keyboard and what they can do. This way, you can confidently program your synth's internal effects, as well as learn the art of working with effects pedals.

There are many ways to alter sound via effects. The following explanations are merely guidelines—there is nothing like experiencing them yourself and tweaking them as you play and learn.

Modulation Effects

There are many types of modulation effects, which are based on the delaying of the initial sound. Each type of effect can be mixed with a certain amount of non-delayed sound to make the effect more or less predominant.

Flanging creates a short delay that modulates the sound in a variety of ways, from a mild gurgling effect to a jet airplane "whoosh." *Phasing* is similar to flanging, but the input and output sounds get crossed, creating a phase effect. *Chorusing* provides depth by adding a short delay to simulate two instruments playing at once. *Echo* is something we're all familiar with—the (often fading) repetition of a sound at regular or irregular intervals. *Vibrato* is a slight and rapid change in pitch, the rich but subtle "wobble" you often hear in the voice of a good singer. *Tremolo* is a slight varying of the amplitude or a very rapid reiteration of a sound (think of a violinist quickly bowing back and forth on a single note), producing an effect that can be similar to vibrato. There are many offshoots of these effects, all with different names but with the same set of general parameters as those mentioned above.

Rate or *speed* here refers to the speed at which a sound is modulated. *Depth, range* or *amount* is the amount of modulation applied to the delay time—the addition of a more "effected" tone to the sound. *Balance, mix* or *blend* determines how much of the delayed/modulated sound is being output; a balance of 100% will give you all effected sound, while a balance of 0% will give you just the basic input (dry) sound. *Feedback, recirculation* or *regeneration* determines how much of the output sound feeds back into the input; the more you feed back in, the heavier the delay (think of echo effects).

All of these effects are available in rack-mountable or pedal forms. Pedals are the devices you see guitarists stepping on and tweaking during a gig. They can be very handy in a live situation when you can use the controls (rate, balance, etc.) to alter the sound at will. Rack effects aren't as easy to fiddle with on the fly, but they are very handy in the MIDI studio. Many rack-effects modules can produce several types of effects at once, such as a chorus plus a delay. They are programmable and usually MIDI-controllable. Most keyboards also come with built-in effects.

Reverb

Reverb is an electronic simulation of an acoustic space; it allows your keyboard to sound as if it were in a large room, a tight closet, a cathedral, etc. It adds depth to tracks and makes them sound more realistic. It is, in short, the most necessary element in a MIDI studio. Most rack units have some sort of reverb built in, and some are dedicated reverb units. When you can't afford to record in a great-sounding room, a dry room with reverb added can create the ambience you need and want.

There are different parameters for reverb. *Type* indicates the kind of reverb— "room," "hall," and "spring" (the classic twangy sound in much music of the 1950s) are among the most popular. *Size* is the size of the room to be emulated. It can be described in cubic meters or cubic feet, or in milliseconds. *Early reflections* are the first sets of echoes you hear, typically after 20–50 milliseconds, while larger values create the feeling of a larger space. *Pre-delay*, like early reflections, controls the time before the reverb begins. *Decay time* controls how long the reverberated sound lasts until it fades away completely. *Mix, balance* or *blend* determines how much of the reverberated sound is output, 100% being all reverberated sound, 0% all dry sound. *Gated reverb* makes the output sound as if it were backwards by using a volume threshold to determine when the sound and reverb are output. This effect has a distinctive sound which was popularized in the 1980s by Peter Gabriel, Phil Collins and many others. There are many other parameters that have different names from manufacturer to manufacturer, and some are more complicated than others. However, they will all have these basic functions.

Compressors/Limiters

Compressors control the peaks and valleys of a recorded piece of music. They can boost the quiet parts and tone down the louder parts to create a more even sound. They can boost the overall level of a track, adding life to an otherwise dull-sounding song, but they can also squeeze the sound into a sonic spectrum that many find unnatural. Either way, a compressor is an essential part of any studio, whether it is used a great deal or only rarely. *Limiters* act in a similar way to compressors, but they flatten all peaks (higher volume levels), leaving lower levels unchanged.

All compressors have a few basic controls. The *threshold* is the level at which the compressor kicks in. A lower threshold triggers the compression at lower levels, while a higher threshold needs a louder level to kick in. *Ratio* is the amount of output level signal change from the input sound. A higher ratio increases the effect of the compression. *Attack* determines how long it takes for the compression to kick in. Longer attack times let more of the natural input sound through without being compressed. *Output control* is the overall volume for the track. It's used to balance the input and output levels to make them equal. *Decay* is the time it takes for the compressor's sound to die away. A longer decay time sounds more natural, while a short decay creates a "whoosh" effect. The *hard knee/soft knee* controls how quickly the compression kicks in. Soft knee slowly brings in the compression once the signal has reached the threshold, while hard knee kicks in the full amount of compression once the threshold is achieved.

There are other settings on some compressors, but these are the basic controls. In general, compression is used during mixdown, where it is applied to certain tracks or to the entire mix. Guitarists and live sound mixers use it to keep the overall level from getting too loud.

Setting Up Your MIDI Studio

So much to buy...this can all seem a little intimidating to one's wallet, but you don't need to go all out when setting up your first studio. Pieces can be acquired one at a time, and there's no need to buy the newest and most expensive piece of gear when you can get something else that will do much the same thing for less. It's a good idea to start out with a small, basic system, since when you're first getting the hang of this, you will learn everything much more quickly from a small setup than from an overwhelming one. First learn how to get a great sound out of next to nothing, then add new gear as you go.

Here's an example of a small MIDI studio setup. Note how the different effects are routed through the mixer's auxiliary ("aux") sends—everything feeds into the mixer and, eventually, into the master recorder.

Possible MIDI Studio Setup

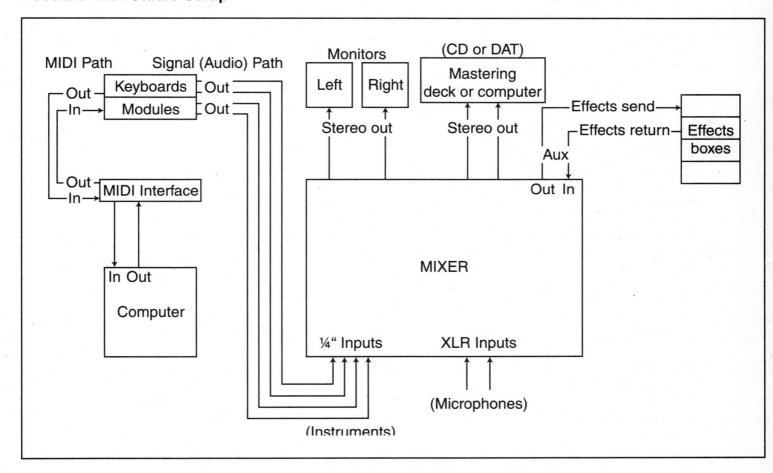

x

Where to Set Up Your MIDI Studio

People have created home studios in closets, garages, and all sorts of other tiny spaces. If you don't have enough room in your home, you can rent a small space somewhere, but it's always a good idea to start small. If you already have a spot where your keyboard rig is set up, then you have a place. A corner makes a good place, as you will be able to get to every piece of gear easily when it is arranged around you in an "L" or "V" formation. As a rule, the gear you need to adjust most should be the most accessible, while gear that you rarely change, like power amps and reverb units, can be placed in a lower or more inaccessible location.

Possible Midi Studio Setup (In a Corner)

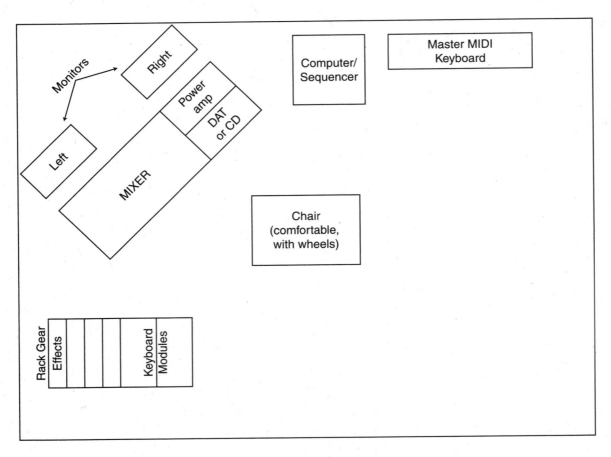

You can set up your studio in any space you see fit, but a basic principle to keep in mind is that the monitors should be facing the farthest point in the room. For example, if you have a narrow room in which to work, your monitors should be facing the far wall, not the near wall.

Possible Midi Studio Setup (Narrow Room)

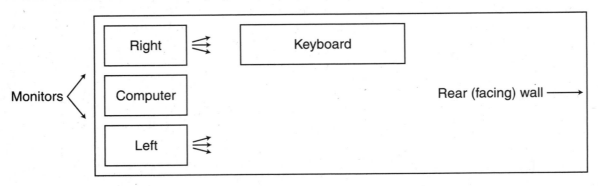

GETTING INTO A BAND

How to Get Into a Band

If you're ready to join a band, you're already well on the way if you can play your instrument with a relatively high degree of skill—and have good hygiene, control of your ego and a positive attitude! If you're fairly new to the music scene, look for bands or musical projects whose members are on roughly the same musical level as, or are slightly better than, you. You'll find that playing with musicians better than you will make you play better as well, and that with them you will be able to do things you didn't think you were capable of. However, being in a band whose abilities are markedly better than yours may cause problems, as one lesser musician can disrupt the entire musical flow of the entire group. In other words, aim high, but not too high.

The role of a keyboard player in bands playing in most contemporary styles does not necessarily require you to be a virtuoso on the keys. Technical wizardry is often the province of other instruments, allowing you to add subtle colors and textures.

Here are some ways to get into a band:

TIPS

1. **Ask your friends.** Seek out friends and acquaintances who are in bands. Put the word out that you are looking for a group situation—you will probably get calls to come and play with a group, or even with just one person with an idea for a band. Having a personal connection is a great advantage. Any sort of recommendation is valuable, especially if you're entering into to a situation about which you know very little.

2. **Scour audition ads.** Look in your local paper—weeklies are usually best—or in music stores for ads placed by bands in search of members. There are always bands looking for someone to join them, either because a member has left, they're still in the process of formation, or they've just decided to add keyboards to their lineup. You can also use the Internet to look for band postings in your area—many on-line music sites have classified ads that should prove helpful.

3. **Do it yourself.** If you have an idea or concept for a band, there's nothing wrong with getting it off the ground on your own. Place an ad in a local paper or ask around. Make clear your intentions for the proposed band, your musical influences and the fact that you're just starting out. It's pointless and detrimental to make false claims—that you have gigs already lined up or that your uncle is a big-shot producer. Even if you *do* have a producer for an uncle, it's better to keep that out of the ad and to keep the focus on the band itself. That way, you'll find people more committed to a start-up project. Remember: You don't necessarily have to be the leader of the group, even if the group is your idea. Ideally a band should be a democratic union in which everyone has an equal say in what the group does.

Auditions

Chances are, you've auditioned for something in your life, whether for a spot on a Little League team or a role in a play. Whatever the situation, you were being judged. Some people have a hard time with this, saying that they don't like to be judged or compared to others, but we judge and compare things every day, from the people we like to the toothpaste we don't. The process of finding the right person for a job—or a band—isn't necessarily unfair; it's just a part of existence.

Setting up an Audition

Most groups auditioning prospective members will want to know specifically about your qualifications to determine whether you're worthy to be in their band. Some will just want to talk to you to see if you're on the same page, musically speaking. Likewise, your first contact with a band or one of its members will be an important factor in helping you decide whether or not you actually want to audition. Be especially attentive and observant, and don't be afraid to ask questions, whether about the band's musical style and goals or about practical issues like equipment, schedules and personnel.

A band in search of a new member should be forthcoming, though not mindlessly boastful, about its background and accomplishments. Be wary of a band that tells you how great their music is but doesn't want you to hear it. At the same time, realize that sometimes band members are suspicious that new people may steal the group's songs.

The band's members will want to get a good idea of what you are like—not only as a musician, but as a person. Half of a band's musical chemistry comes from the personal chemistry among the members. It's best to be truthful, and at the same time not to brag. Don't say that you've traveled around the world and played for thousands of people if you haven't. Even if you have done those things, you don't necessarily need to trumpet them, at least not right away. You can always share more of your background—and amusing anecdotes—*after* you get the gig.

Some bands will ask what you look like, your age and other personal questions. They are likely interested in how you will fit in with the band's image. Despite all you hear about horrible, messy band breakups, many groups, both famous and obscure, have existed for years (even decades) because they have worked well together on several levels. Discovering as much about prospective members as possible is obviously a band's key to finding—and keeping—good, valuable personnel.

Getting Ready for an Audition

Let's say you've been given a time slot to audition with the band, or at least some of its members. If the band has given you a recording of their music to study, learn it as thoroughly as possible. If the band has a vocalist, it's a good idea to know the lyrics at key points (e.g., the last line before the chorus or any other spot that will cue a transition), especially if you have to change sounds or get ready for a more complicated part. Knowing the lyrics also earns you brownie points from the lyricist, since so many of them claim that nobody pays attention to lyrics these days.

Before you leave home, make sure all of your gear is in good working order and that you have everything you need. It's a drag to ask a stranger for a spare cable, and it mars your image as a professional. Arrive at the audition at least 15 minutes early. If you are bringing your own equipment, such as keyboards and amplification, set up whatever you can beforehand. The less time you take to get ready in the audition itself, the more time you will have to play.

During the Audition

If you have any questions about chords or forms in a tune, ask the band before you play. When you run through the songs for the first time, listen carefully, as the music may differ from how it sounds in the recording. Ask about this, and they will most probably be happy to explain—and will appreciate your attentive ear. You can be sure that in every case, playing the songs live will feel different from playing with the recording. Play with confidence, not too loudly and not too quietly. Be sincerely apologetic about anything you may not know or any mistakes you may make, but avoid saying "I'm sorry" repeatedly. If you later find out that you didn't get the gig for one reason or another, politely ask one or more of the members why—you may gain insight into what to do differently at your next audition. If you don't get the gig, learn from the experience—and realize that the more you audition, the more comfortable you'll feel doing it.

Earl "Bud" Powell, an important bebop innovator, set the standard for modern jazz keyboard soloing in the 1940s.

PHOTO • LYDIA CRISS/COURTESY OF STAR FILE PHOTO, INC

REHEARSING AND GIGGING WITH A BAND

Rehearsal Tips

What do you do once you've made it into a band or put together one of your own? Let's assume you have all the musical slots filled: guitar, bass, drums, vocals (in some cases) and of course keyboards. You need a place to rehearse. What are your options?

Where to Rehearse With Your Band

TIPS

1. **A garage (or basement, etc.).** Make no mistake: Great bands have been born in garage rehearsal spaces. Classic tracks like The Kingsmen's *Louie, Louie* were recorded in a garage; some just sound as though they were. One of the great advantages of a rehearsal space like this is that it's generally free. One drawback, however, is that most garages were built to store cars, lawnmowers and tools—not for optimum acoustic value. Still, the relative isolation of a garage may go far in alleviating one important problem you may encounter elsewhere: disturbing others with your rehearsals. Of course, neighbors will appreciate your consideration when it comes to volume levels and the time of day you rehearse.

   In a garage rehearsal situation you will have to furnish some sort of amplification for anyone who might need it. Vocalists sound best amplified through a PA or similar system rather than through a cheap guitar amp. The better everyone can hear everyone else, the better the rehearsal will be.

   Some basements will make an excellent place to rehearse, provided that they are dry, uncluttered (allowing you plenty of space), and that whoever lives above doesn't mind the noise (or isn't home).

2. **A rehearsal studio.** Most areas of the country have rehearsal studios that musicians can rent; look for ads in the phone book or in local newspapers with good music coverage. Both hourly and monthly rentals are generally available. In the case of hourly rentals, there will generally be some kind of sound system in the room, along with a drum set and amps for bass and guitar players. Not all studios will have these elements, so call around to see what is available.

   Rental studios range from foul-smelling, postage stamp–sized dumps to beautiful, great-sounding places that are nice enough to live in. Rates will vary according to location, size, and amenities. Be aware that a space that seems like a deal may not be at all suitable for your needs. Check out a studio ahead of time, paying close attention to factors like soundproofing, cleanliness and air quality—all of these can have a direct impact on your rehearsals. Try to hear another band rehearse in the same space, and listen for sounds bleeding in from other rooms. If you can't look at a particular studio ahead of time, ask around to find out if anyone you know has rehearsed there before. A solid recommendation from someone you trust is the next best thing to seeing it for yourself.

Monthly Rehearsal Spaces

If your band is really serious about rehearsing two or three times a week, it can be a good idea to go in together on a space that is yours alone. With space that is exclusive, you can rehearse at any time, customize it according to your needs and tastes, and use it to store your instruments and equipment. You will of course have to supply your own amps, sound system, etc. , but you will save money in the long run compared to the cost of hourly studio rentals. Keep in mind that you may want to be sure that the band will work out before investing time and money in a place of your own, so an hourly space may be a good bet as you start out.

DID YOU KNOW?

Major "Big Maceo" Merriweather came up during the boogie-woogie craze and went on to become one of the most popular blues artists on the Chicago scene in the 1940s. His piano style was hugely influential to the young pianists coming up in Chicago, most notably two of Muddy Waters's pianists: Little Johnny Jones and Otis Spann. Merriweather both sang and played, and his songs were mainly his own, many of them in the sixteen-bar blues form. His best-known song is Worried Life Blues, which borrows a verse from guitarist Sleepy John Estes. Merriweather's first recording session took place in 1941, and unfortunately, his last was in 1945. Shortly after that time, he suffered a paralyzing stroke, and though he recovered from it, his playing never reached its previous level. The 1945 session produced Merriweather's solo masterpiece, "Chicago Breakdown," a classic example of boogie-woogie piano at its finest.

photo • bill greensmith/COURTESY OF STAR FILE PHOTO, INC

178 Making A Demo Recording

Most club owners and bookers will want to hear some sort of recording of your band before they book you. With the price of manufacturing CDs continuing to drop, it is becoming easier and more economical to produce a recording of your own. CDs are also the best medium for the listener, as it is simple to skip from track to track. Most people who book venues won't have time to listen to a demo recording all the way through, so here are some guidelines to ensure that your music will be heard and appreciated:

TIPS

1. **Don't go overboard.** A band's first demo need not be a full studio recording. One easy way to record your band is to set up two identical microphones in front of the group. Position the mikes at ear level and about as far apart from one another as your own ears to capture the sound close to the way one would hear it in person.

   Place the amps and instruments at equal distances from the microphones and record the band playing through one song. Listen to the playback to judge the overall balance and clarity. Reposition the players or microphones as needed.

2. **Don't include too many songs.** When you've finished recording all the band's songs, pick the three or four that sound best. A demo should be a sonic résumé, an encapsulation of the band's style, sound and skills. It's a good idea to make the first track a quick, attention-getting song—your best one, if possible. This will grab the listener's attention and make him/her want to listen to more. Place slower, more lyrical songs in the middle, and end the demo on a high note with another upbeat, ear-catching number. Take the listener on a trip through your band's sound.

3. **Edit carefully.** You don't want the listener to hear comments made between takes, so leave ample silence both before and after each track as you record. This will make it easier to edit the recording and to burn CDs. Leave about three to four seconds between songs on the final master. This will give the listener time to prepare for the next tune.

4. **Present an attractive product.** There's no greater turn-off to a booker or agent than a recording that looks cheap or cheesy. With the availability of so many desktop graphics programs, a sharp-looking cover is easy to make and good for your image. A photograph of the band, the higher the quality the better, is also beneficial. The demo doesn't have to be shrink-wrapped or even in a CD jewel case, but the better your band looks, the more positive and professional an impact you'll make.

Make sure the demo *really* captures your band—it should feel and sound like a good recording of your band playing live. The entire package should present the band as it really is. A band trying to make itself seem "bigger" than it really is is usually easy to spot, and a shoddily produced demo with poor production and graphics gives the game away even faster.

Getting Gigs for the Band

Assuming you've got the band together and have at least 45 minutes' worth of music to play, you're ready to start gigging. Now the question is, "How do we get gigs?" You've probably already seen other bands perform in clubs or other venues. If you haven't, go now! This is the best way to know who's out there and what they're playing. Look for bands that seem to have a musical approach similar to yours and meet them if you can. Often, a recommendation to a club from another band will help you get gigs.

Once you've heard other bands and become familar with a number of venues, you should have a pretty good idea of the kind of club where your music would fit in. When you discover a place you particularly like, find out who handles entertainment bookings there and deal with him or her directly. You should have the attitude of a professional when you approach the person in charge. Have all necessary information (availability, etc.) at the ready, ask thoughtful, pertinent questions and be prepared to succinctly describe the band's style and performance experience.

So you've got a gig. Now what do you do? First, make sure that the whole band can actually make the gig. It's a real drag, not to mention a poor reflection on the band, to cancel any engagement, no matter what the circumstances. One near-certain result of a cancellation is that you'll be less likely to be booked at a venue again. Once it is clear that everyone can make the gig, how do you ensure that everything is ready? Here are a few pointers:

TIPS

1. **Assemble a tight, cohesive set.** The club will let you know exactly how much time you have to perform. For a typical club gig of 45 minutes, you can assume that around 10 songs will cover the time allotted. Make a set list. Start with something that grabs people's attention, something that isn't terribly slow. As a rule, never play two slow songs in a row, or more than two songs that are in the same key or are similar in style or tempo. Your last song should be powerful and catchy so that when people leave, the sound of it will remain in their ears.

   In your last rehearsal before the gig, play your set list in order and carefully time the total length, making sure that it is no longer than the time allowed for your set. Many clubs are very strict about time limits, and some are downright rude if you exceed your allotted time. If anything, make your set shorter than the time allowed; that way, you'll have time to play everything if a guitarist's string breaks or some other unexpected situation arises. If there is time left at the end, you can always fit in an extra song or two. Have an encore prepared just in case, but don't always expect to perform it; time constraints or audience apathy may dictate a quick exit.

2. **Make sure your equipment is in good working order.** Whether or not you're able to have a sound check (which will not be possible at some clubs), make sure beforehand that all of your cables, disks, keyboards, amplifiers, etc. are in proper working order. Do a complete "idiot check" of your gear before you leave for the gig. Know exactly what you will need, including how many cables. It's better to bring too much equipment than too little. Don't take a chance on iffy gear. If a cable doesn't appear to be working well, leave it at home and buy a new one.

3. **Don't be nervous. Don't be cocky.** It's natural that you'll be nervous to some degree, especially at your first gigs, but try not to show it onstage. Channel your nervous energy into the performance. One sure cure (or at least effective treatment) for nervousness is thorough preparation. Make sure you feel good about all the music you are to play before you go onstage. Conversely, too much ego onstage will seem like a self-tribute, and most people, especially those in the record business, will see right through it. Stage presence is great, but contrived theatrics usually come off as unprofessional and ill-conceived.

4. **Be on time.** "On time" usually means being at the gig at least 30 minutes before you are to begin playing. This gives you enough time to make sure everything is ready: the setup, set list, etc. This will also ensure that you'll feel comfortable with your surroundings during the gig. Note that some places will want you there even earlier for a sound check, which is something you'll want to take advantage of. You'll be able to set up your equipment before the gig, perform the sound check and be able to leave most of the setup in place for the actual performance.

UNDERSTANDING THE MUSIC BUSINESS

The problem with the music business is that it is a business. Not all musicians are inclined toward business-related and creative matters in equal measure. Unfortunately, so many musicians have been ripped off by unscrupulous business people that it is now necessary for musicians to have a good idea of how the music business works as a whole. There are so many aspects to the music business that it is difficult to cover them all, but here are some basic concepts to get you started.

Gigs and Contracts

If you are booking a gig for yourself, it is often a good idea to use a contract in dealing with your client. Your contract should outline exactly what you will need from the venue and what the venue will expect from you. Each point should be spelled out as clearly and succinctly as possible so that there won't be any questions or problems later. Make sure you get the contract to the client at least 2½ weeks before the event, and ask that it be signed and returned immediately.

A contract signed by both parties binds you and the other person(s) to fulfill all its terms and conditions. If you do not meet all the terms and conditions, the other party has the right to not pay you in full or to take you to court. However, you have the same right and can refuse to play if basic agreements are not met when you arrive at the venue. Most musicians will allow a certain leeway on some issues, such as only having three monitors onstage instead of four. Small issues can be overlooked, and they don't necessarily justify a refusal to play. However, a signed contract allows you to seek a remedy if important criteria are not met.

Not every gig will require the use of a contract. Many small clubs and restaurants don't work with contracts, since they change the entertainment frequently, and there is rarely enough money involved to warrant the time it takes to prepare contracts. Of course, be sure that the club or venue has a good reputation and has not cancelled gigs or refused to pay a band after a gig—unless there was a legitimate reason for doing so.

Here is a sample contract for a private party or wedding gig. You can use this as a template to create your own contract, adding or subtracting points as necessary. Anywhere you see text underlines, just replace it with your own information.

(Your name, address, phone number, fax number and e-mail address here)

Dear John Doe,

This contract will confirm our engagement to provide music for your wedding reception to be held on June 17 in the year 2010 beginning at 7:00 p.m. We will play the equivalent of 3 sets of 50 minutes each between the hours of 7:00 p.m. and 10:00 p.m. with two short breaks of 10 minutes each, during which we will provide recorded music. Our attire will be suits and our repertoire will consist of see attached list. The band consists of Steven Jones, keyboards; Bill Smith, guitar; John Brown, bass; Thomas Miller, percussion.

As agreed, I will provide the following equipment: all musical equipment, PA system, recorded music during breaks.

You will provide the following equipment: sheltered playing area, electrical power.

Food and drink of the same quality provided to your guests will also be provided for the band *[note here whether the band is to be fed free of charge, are subject to a cash bar, etc.].* It is to be made clear to the caterer and/or staff at the venue that the band members are to be treated as your guests. *[These items are pertinent mainly if you are playing a gig at which is food is to be served. Note that if your band consists of more than eight people, it may be difficult to get the client to agree to a "free food" arrangement.]*

Our fee for this engagement will be $800.00, which includes all transportation costs. To activate this agreement I must receive a nonrefundable deposit of $80.00 by June 3, 2010. The balance is to be paid to me immediately following the engagement. If overtime is required, and if other obligations do not prevent us from continuing our performance, the rate is $150.00 per half hour, or any fragment thereof.

In case of injury or illness, at my sole discretion I reserve the right to replace any member of my group to ensure the quality of performance you have requested. Please make sure that we are advised of any special song requests well in advance. If you have more than one special request, additional rehearsal costs will apply. Also, please make sure to provide us with adequate directions to the engagement at least two (2) weeks in advance.

Please sign and immediately return both copies of this agreement to me along with the deposit. I will countersign and immediately send one copy to you for your files. If the deposit is in the form of a check, please make it payable to Steven Jones.

If you should have any further questions, feel free to contact me via the information above.

Sincerely,

Steven Jones

Accepted by (X) _____ dated February 1, 2010

Address_____

Telephone _____   Email_____

The Recording Industry

At the dawn of the 21st century, the music business is in a strange state of flux. Technology is changing everything so fast that information quickly goes out of date. Some people think that record companies as they currently exist may become a thing of the past in a few years. Many people are creating their own music from start to finish and marketing it over the Internet, achieving sales without the help (or hindrance) of record companies. It is impossible to predict what the future holds for the music business.

Currently, the major record companies are the biggest manufacturers and distributors of recorded music. They essentially function as banks. When you sign a contract with a record label, you will receive a loan that pays for recording, promotion, distribution and tour expenses. The label will also give you an advance—money to cover your living expenses and studio time. The good thing about an advance is that if your recording doesn't earn enough to cover this amount, you don't have to pay it back. On the downside, the label will probably drop you, and other companies may be afraid to pick you up.

You really don't earn anything from a recording until it sells enough copies to cover the company's investment in you, including your advance. If the recording recoups this initial investment—which does not always happen—the earnings from that point are divided between you, the record company and others (the producer, for example). Hopefully, your contract will assign you a healthy percentage of these profits—your royalties.

The Record Deal

When you sign a contract with a record label, it is an exclusive deal, which means that you will not be able to record for any other labels or projects without the record company's permission. Labels will often try to sign you to a multi-record deal. A lot of new artists are offered a five- or six-record deal, but this is not necessarily a good thing, as there is no guarantee that your label will actually put out every album—or even your first one. The streets of major cities are overrun with musicians and bands that signed a deal with a label only to be dropped from the label even after making a recording (and some don't get that far). Record companies can entangle you in red tape, keeping you entirely out of the loop as to what they plan on doing with you. Labels want to sign you to multi-record deals because if you do well, they will have a contract with you that keeps you tied to the deal—which, in turn, makes them more money. Sound evil? It sure can be.

The main reason to play music is to express yourself artistically and emotionally—not to make all the money you can, though that is a nice benefit. If you want a large, guaranteed income, don't look to a record contract to fulfill that dream. So, how *do* you actually make money with recorded music? Aside from earning royalties or performing live in support of a recording, there are other ways to generate income:

TIPS

1. **Publishing.** If you want to write music only for yourself or your band to perform, you will probably just need a publishing company of your own. You will need to set this up through both a performing rights organization (ASCAP, BMI or SESAC) and the government. Starting up a publishing company usually means incorporating yourself in some way. A knowledgeable and trustworthy lawyer may be well worth the expense to ensure that all legal bases are covered.

   If your goal is to write songs for other people, you might want to try to get a publishing deal with a major publishing company. The goal of this plan is to place your songs on as many albums as possible and thus make as much money as possible. If your record label's publishing company insists on owning part of your songs—something you should aggressively resist—make sure that they don't cross-collateralize your publishing and recording accounts. Cross-collateralization means that a record company can deduct monies from your publishing proceeds if your record sales are not as high as expected.

2. Merchandising. Most of us have t-shirts or posters of bands or artists we like, and a lot of the money spent on these goes to the artist(s). Record companies might try to take control of your merchandising, but if you control it yourself, the profit margin can be very high. A t-shirt with your band's logo might cost just five dollars to make, but you can sell it for 10 or 20 dollars. The only costs to you should be those involved in manufacturing and selling your merchandise.

Promotion and Distribution

If you have a recording of your music, you want to get it out for everyone to hear, right? This may involve the services of a distribution company. The major labels and their subsidiaries all have their own distribution companies or rely on a larger, outside distribution company to put their products on the street. Small and independent labels use independent distributors to get their stuff out there. Some will use one distributor for one part of the country or the world and another for a different area, according to a distributor's strengths in certain markets. Distributors take a portion of your profits for this service. While it should guarantee that your recording will be in major stores nationwide, it doesn't guarantee that it will be advertised. This is where promotion comes in. A record company or distributor will market a type of music to an area that would be likely to favor a certain CD; for instance, country music is promoted more heavily in the South, while R&B is promoted more heavily in urban areas. While this may seem like stereotyping, the figures don't lie—certain types of recordings do sell better in certain areas than others.

A promoter will hype your record for a fee and try to spark interest in it. The best promotions are those in connection with performances by you and your band. A successful promotion makes the public aware of your music through advertising in print, radio, TV and other media. It costs more to hire a promoter, but it can be worth it if you achieve greater sales.

Lawyers

Unfortunately, lawyers are a necessity in the music business, but a good one on your side can get you a good record deal. Labels look at you first as a potential profit-making enterprise, not as a great band or musician that everyone should hear. An entertainment lawyer who works for you in securing the best deal possible is a valuable asset. Be sure you at least get a lawyer you trust to review a record contract before you sign it. Recording (and often, other music-related) contracts are full of legalese and mumbo jumbo. Your lawyer should be able to explain each item in a contract in clear English.

The Shape of Things to Come

In the end, many people take a piece of the financial pie that your music generates. It may seem unfair, but it is the system you're stuck with for the time being. The record industry has been run like this for decades, but there is a ray of hope in the rights that artists have won in the past few years. The continuing evolution of on-line commerce, the rise of file-sharing technologies and services like Napster, the regular introduction of all-new media, and musicians (like Prince, for example) who bypass major labels in producing and distributing their music all suggest that artists are posed to become a more powerful force in the business end of the recording industry than ever before.

GETTING A MANAGER

It's ideal to have someone represent you as an artist. If you have just started out as a band or as a solo artist, you will do fine booking gigs on your own, but as your career progresses you may find it necessary to obtain a manager. This person should not be in the band, but should have a close connection to the band. He or she should have good business sense, with a good idea of how the music business works. This manager could be a friend of the band, someone recommended to you by another band or someone whose opinion you trust in general. In any case, there are a number of things that any good manager should do:

1. **Book gigs—ideally, increasingly better gigs— for you**

2. **Make sure you are paid for each gig**

3. **Scout around for (and stimulate) interest from record companies**

4. **Protect your interests in business dealings**

5. **Take care of business in general so that you can concentrate on your music**

Here's a list of qualities and qualifications a manager should possess:

TIPS

1. **A manager should be friendly but firm.** Someone too hard-headed will turn people off, while someone too soft won't command respect (and will probably get you gigs that no one else wants to do).

2. **A manager should be knowledgeable about many aspects of the music business.** The music business gets more and more confusing and difficult to navigate every day, so the more a manager knows—about contracts, bookings, record deals, etc.—the better off you'll be and the more you'll be able to focus on your music. If you or your manager are in doubt about any aspect of the business, there are many books available that go into the finer points. Be sure to get up-to-date information, as the industry changes so quickly that a five-year-old book is essentially out of date. You can always track down information on the Internet, but be sure to look at official sites—not, for instance, one created by a disgruntled crank who was kicked out of a band 20 years ago.

3. **A manager should be accessible.** "Accessible" in this case means simply that if your manager isn't traveling with you, you should still be able to reach him or her within minutes—via e-mail, telephone, fax or some other means. You'll find that communication with your manager at a moment's notice is indispensable, whether he or she is negotiating a contract for you in Los Angeles (while you're in New York), or you're stuck in a blizzard in Peoria and don't know how you're going to make it to your next gig.

4. **Above all, a manager should be trustworthy.** If a manager brags about cheating someone else in order to get you better gigs, who's to say he or she won't cheat you as well? Donald Passman, noted music lawyer and author of several books on the music industry, has pointed out that someone who keeps telling you how honest he or she is usually isn't honest at all. Ask to review your manager's business records from time to time, and make certain that you are constantly updated on any new deals. You should know *exactly* where all your money comes from. If your manager hedges or procrastinates in telling you, ask pointed questions—and reevaluate your association with him or her. Unscrupulous managers have cheated many musicians out of their hard-earned money. Managers like these will always try to explain or justify why your money has "disappeared." Become as familiar as you can with the different aspects of the music business so you can ask your manager specific questions—and will know when you're being cheated.

What to Expect from a Manager

Your manager should have more contacts in the business than you do. Otherwise, what do you have to gain from the relationship? In terms of fees, a manager will typically ask for 10–20% of the overall gross on any money *he or she makes for you.* This latter point (in italics) is particularly important—any money you make on your own should not be taken by your manager as a fee. Many managers will want you to let them handle *all* bookings and business deals. This is fine, but only if the manager has your complete trust.

In general, a manager should not ask for money up front except in the case of small expenses related directly to you or the band. Giving a manager money up front will never ensure gigs or contracts, but an ideal manager will use his or her contacts in the music industry to get you publicity—and, hopefully, gigs and recording contracts.

A manager should not take a large percentage of the gross pay for a gig if it's under a certain amount. A typical bar or club gig will not pay much, and if a manager takes a cut of this, you will be left with a very paltry sum. It's best to agree on a set fee that the manager will receive for booking low-paying gigs. This has the added benefit of encouraging the manager to book better gigs for you, if only out of self-interest. A manager should not be paid for any gigs, contracts, etc. that were in place before he or she came into the picture. However, if a manager can obtain a better deal for you at a venue where you've already been booked or on a pre-existing contract, he or she should certainly be given some form of compensation.

DID YOU KNOW?

Over the course of five decades, *Keith Jarrett* has moved with ease between the worlds of jazz and classical music. His exceptional talent as an improviser is evident in recordings that range from the famous *The Köln Concert* to the piano concerti of Mozart.

PHOTO • COURTESY OF THE INSTITUTE OF JAZZ STUDIES

PART 4: REFERENCE

This section of the book is provided as a resource for your on-going use. It includes nine basic chords in every key, and an explanation of chord inversions. Starting on page 204, you'll find major scale fingerings in every key and then fingerings for three types of minor scales, also in every key. Finally, on page 224, there is a brief explanation of the circle of 5ths, an important musical concept. Enjoy!

CHORD REFERENCE

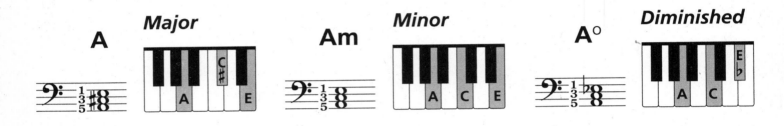

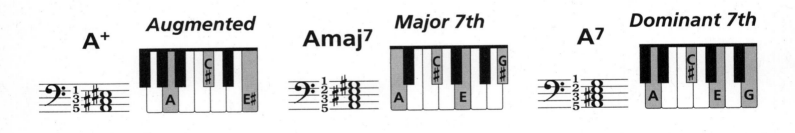

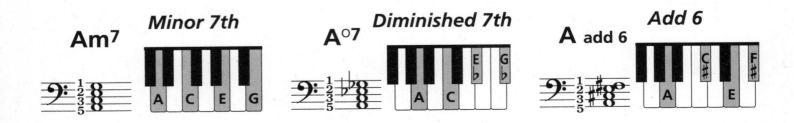

A#

A# *Major*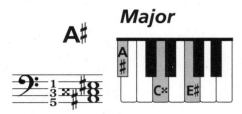

A#m *Minor*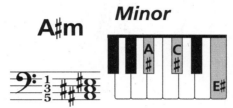

A#° *Diminished*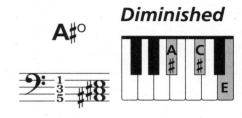

A#+ *Augmented*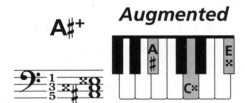

A#maj7 *Major 7th*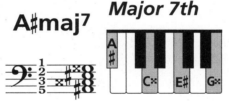

A#7 *Dominant 7th*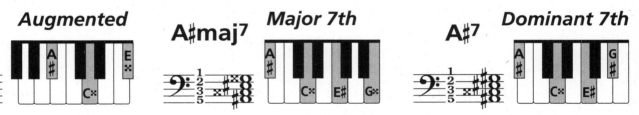

A#m7 *Minor 7th*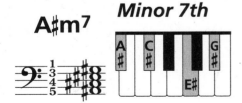

A#°7 *Diminished 7th*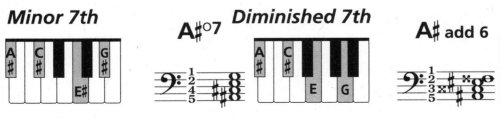

A# add 6 *Add 6*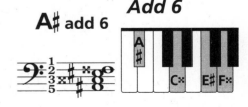

B

Major
B

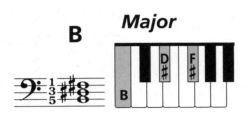

Minor
Bm

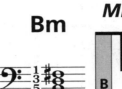
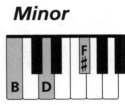

Diminished
B°

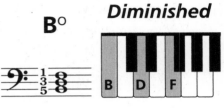

Augmented
B+

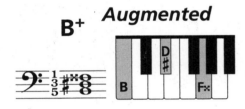

Major 7th
Bmaj7

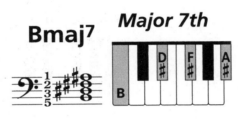

Dominant 7th
B7

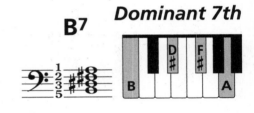

Minor 7th
Bm7

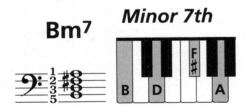

Diminished 7th
B°7

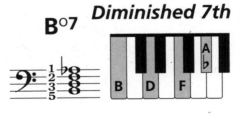

Add 6
B add 6

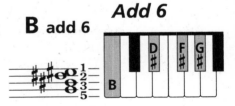

C

C *Major*
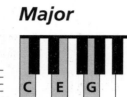

Cm *Minor*

C° *Diminished*
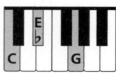
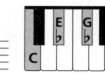

C⁺ *Augmented*

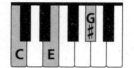

Cmaj⁷ *Major 7th*

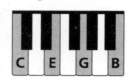

C⁷ *Dominant 7th*

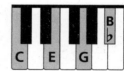

Cm⁷ *Minor 7th*

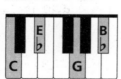

C°⁷ *Diminished 7th*
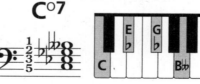

Cadd 6 *Add 6*

C#

C# *Major*

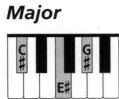

C#m *Minor*

C#° *Diminished*
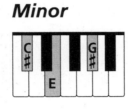
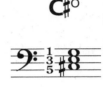
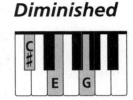

C#+ *Augmented*
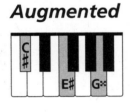

C#maj7 *Major 7th*

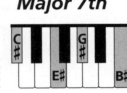

C#7 *Dominant 7th*
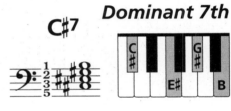

C#m7 *Minor 7th*
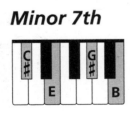

C#°7 *Diminished 7th*
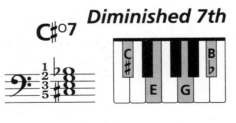

C# add 6 *Add 6*
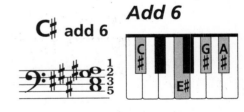

D♭

D♭ *Major*
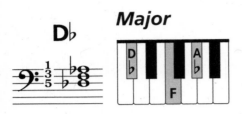

D♭m *Minor*
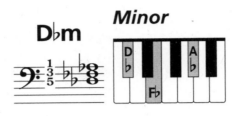

D♭° *Diminished*
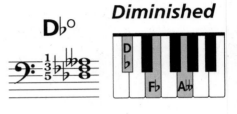

D♭+ *Augmented*
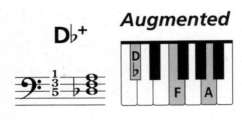

D♭maj⁷ *Major 7th*
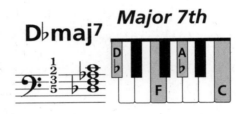

D♭7 *Dominant 7th*
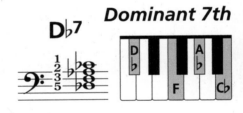

D♭m⁷ *Minor 7th*
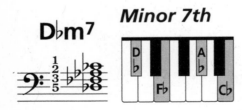

D♭°7 *Diminished 7th*
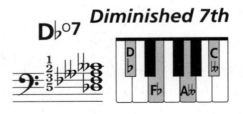

D♭ add 6 *Add 6*
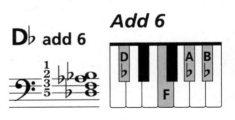

D

Major
D

Minor
Dm

Diminished
D°

Augmented
D⁺

Major 7th
Dmaj⁷
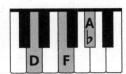

Dominant 7th
D⁷

Minor 7th
Dm⁷

Diminished 7th
D°⁷
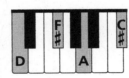

Add 6
D add 6

D♯

D♯   *Major*

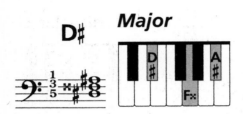

D♯m   *Minor*

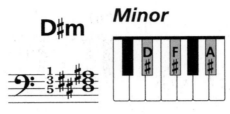

D♯°   *Diminished*

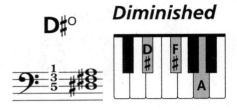

D♯+   *Augmented*

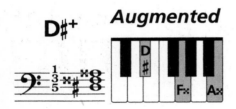

D♯maj⁷   *Major 7th*

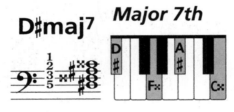

D♯7   *Dominant 7th*

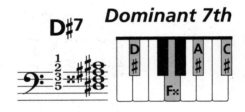

D♯m⁷   *Minor 7th*

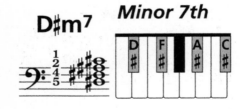

D♯°7   *Diminished 7th*

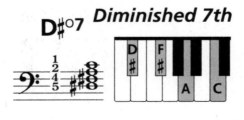

D♯ add 6   *Add 6*

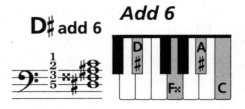

Major
Eb

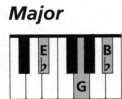

Minor

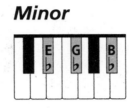

Diminished
Ebo

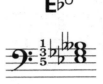
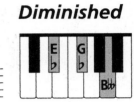

Augmented
Eb+

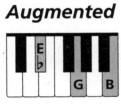

Major 7th
Ebmaj7

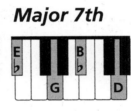

Dominant 7th
Eb7

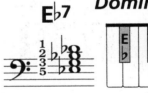
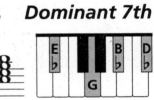

Minor 7th
Ebm7

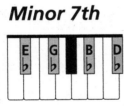

Diminished 7th
Ebo7

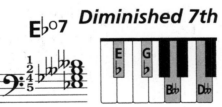

Add 6
Eb add 6

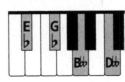
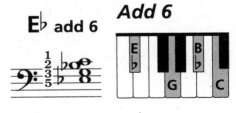

E

E — Major

Em — Minor
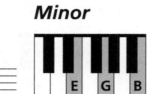

E° — Diminished

E+ — Augmented
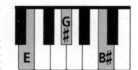

Emaj7 — Major 7th

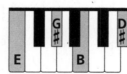

E7 — Dominant 7th

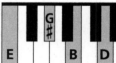

Em7 — Minor 7th

E°7 — Diminished 7th

E add 6 — Add 6

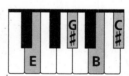

F

F *Major*
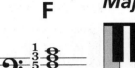 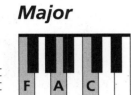

Fm *Minor*
 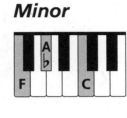

F° *Diminished*
 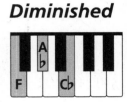

F+ *Augmented*
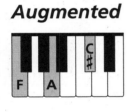

Fmaj7 *Major 7th*

F7 *Dominant 7th*
 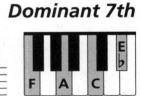

Fm7 *Minor 7th*
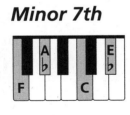

F°7 *Diminished 7th*
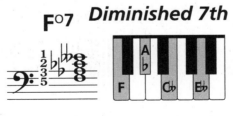

F add 6 *Add 6*
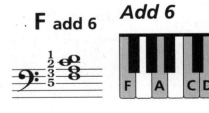

F#

F#   *Major*
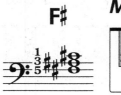

F#m   *Minor*
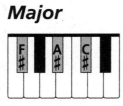

F#°   *Diminished*

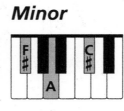

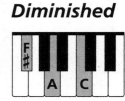

F#+   *Augmented*

F#maj7   *Major 7th*
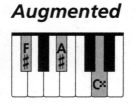

F#7   *Dominant 7th*

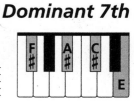

F#m7   *Minor 7th*

F#°7   *Diminished 7th*
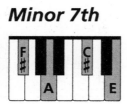

F# add 6   *Add 6*
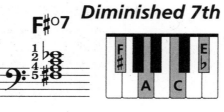

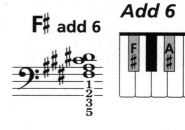

G♭

G♭ **Major**

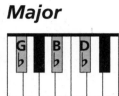

G♭m **Minor**

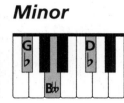

G♭° **Diminished**

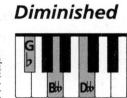

G♭+ **Augmented**

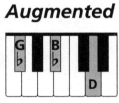

G♭maj7 **Major 7th**
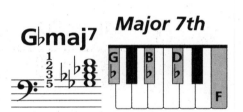

G♭7 **Dominant 7th**
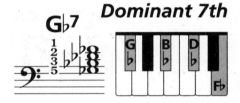

G♭m7 **Minor 7th**

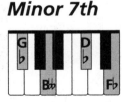

G♭°7 **Diminished 7th**
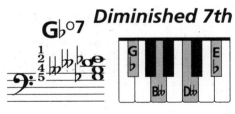

G♭ add 6 **Add 6**
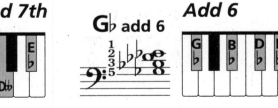

G

G *Major*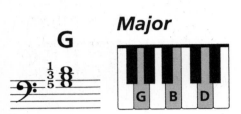

Gm *Minor*

G° *Diminished*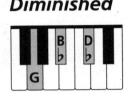

G⁺ *Augmented*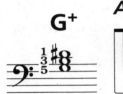

Gmaj⁷ *Major 7th*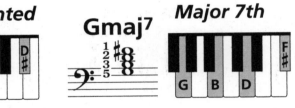

G⁷ *Dominant 7th*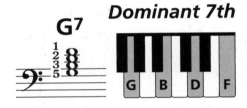

Gm⁷ *Minor 7th*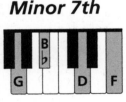

G°⁷ *Diminished 7th*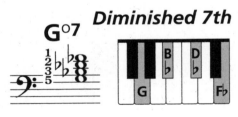

G add 6 *Add 6*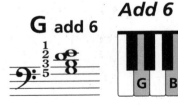

G#

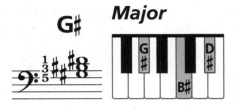

G# — *Major*

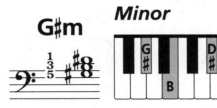

G#m — *Minor*

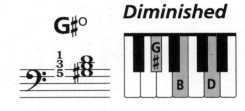

G#° — *Diminished*

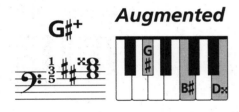

G#+ — *Augmented*

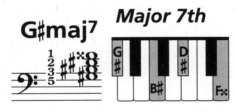

G#maj7 — *Major 7th*

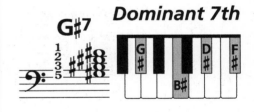

G#7 — *Dominant 7th*

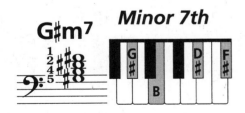

G#m7 — *Minor 7th*

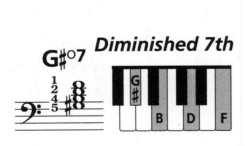

G#°7 — *Diminished 7th*

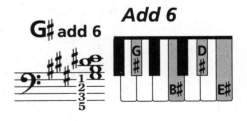

G# add 6 — *Add 6*

A♭

A♭ *Major*

A♭m *Minor*

A♭° *Diminished*
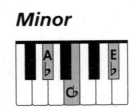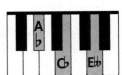

A♭+ *Augmented*

A♭maj7 *Major 7th*

A♭7 *Dominant 7th*
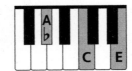

A♭m7 *Minor 7th*

A♭°7 *Diminished 7th*

A♭ add 6 *Add 6*
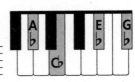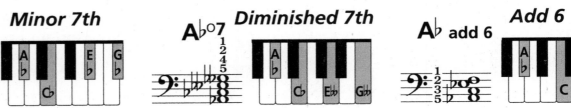

Inverting Chords

All of the chords on pages 186–202 are shown in *root position*. Any root position chord may be changed by moving the root (bottom note) of the chord to another position. This is called an *inversion*—it means the notes are rearranged and a note other than the root is the bottom note of the chord.

First Inversion

The first inversion of a C triad can be made by moving the root (C) to the top of the chord.

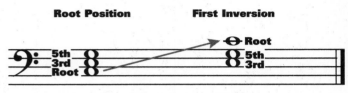

C E G becomes E G C

All letter names are the same, but the 3rd (E) is now on the bottom, and the root (C) is now on top. This is called *first inversion*.

Second Inversion

Any first inversion chord may be inverted again by moving the lowest note (3rd) to the top.

The second inversion can made from a first inversion C chord by moving the 3rd (E) to the top of the chord.

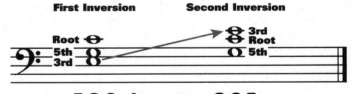

E G C becomes G C E

All letter names are the same, but the 5th (G) is now on the bottom, and the root (C) is now in the middle. This is called *second inversion*.

Inverting Four-Note Chords

Four-note chords such as 7th chords can also be inverted. Chords with four notes can be written in four different positions: root position, first inversion, second inversion and third inversion.

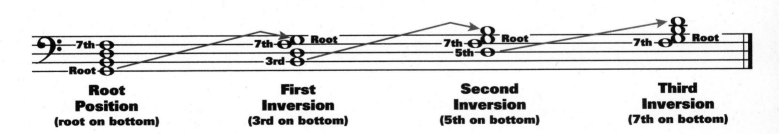

MAJOR SCALES

C Major Scale

G Major Scale

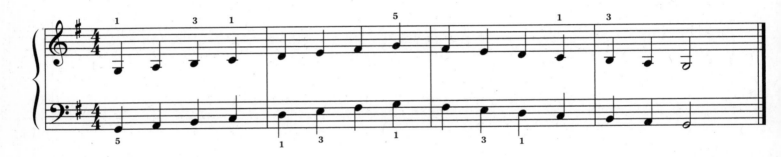

D Major Scale

A Major Scale

E Major Scale

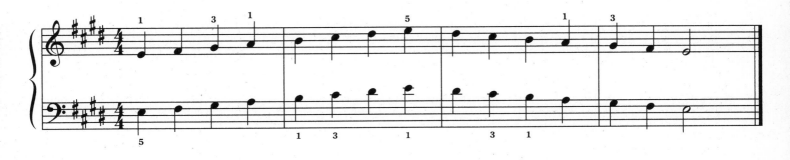

B Major Scale

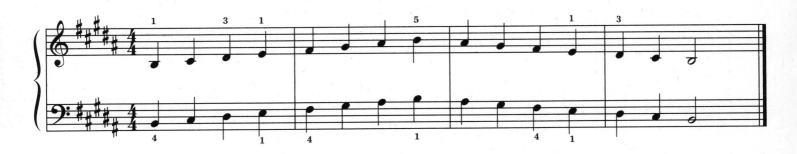

F# Major Scale

C# Major Scale

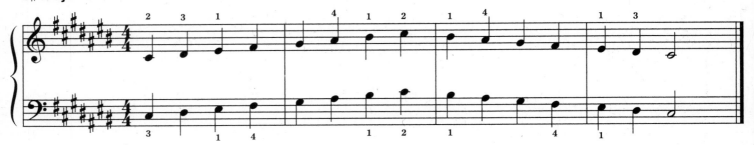

F Major Scale

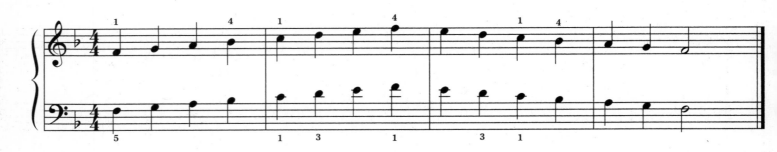

B♭ Major Scale

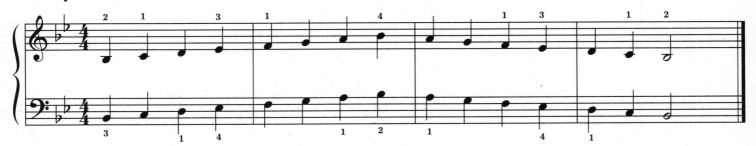

E♭ Major Scale

A♭ Major Scale

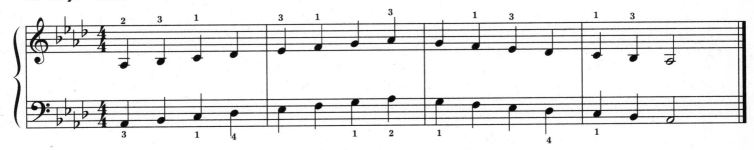

D♭ Major Scale

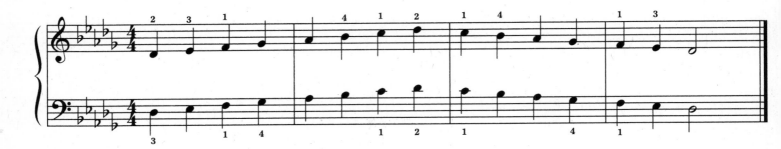

G♭ Major Scale

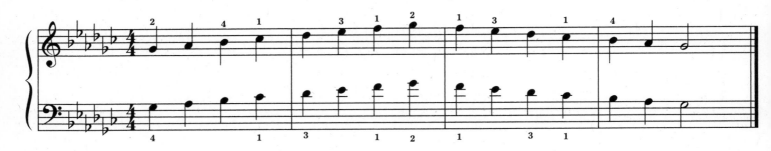

C♭ Major Scale

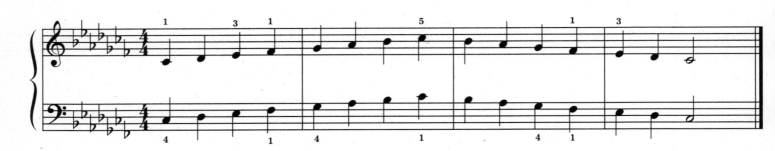

MINOR SCALES

A Natural Minor Scale

A Harmonic Minor Scale

A Melodic Minor Scale

E Natural Minor Scale

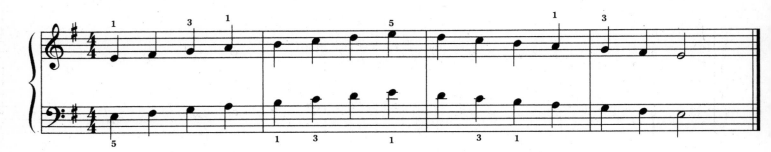

E Harmonic Minor Scale

E Melodic Minor Scale

B Natural Minor Scale

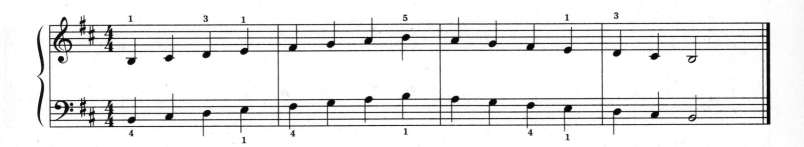

B Harmonic Minor Scale

B Melodic Minor Scale

F♯ Natural Minor Scale

F♯ Harmonic Minor Scale

F♯ Melodic Minor Scale

C# Natural Minor Scale

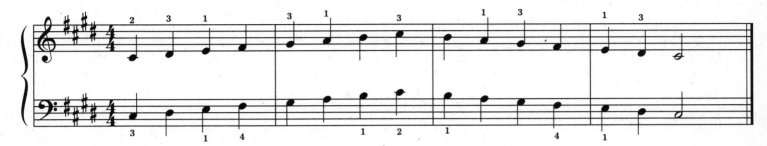

C# Harmonic Minor Scale

C# Melodic Minor Scale

214

G♯ Natural Minor Scale

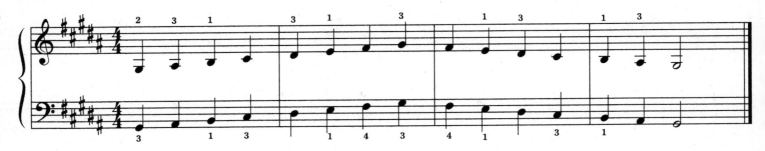

G♯ Harmonic Minor Scale

G♯ Melodic Minor Scale

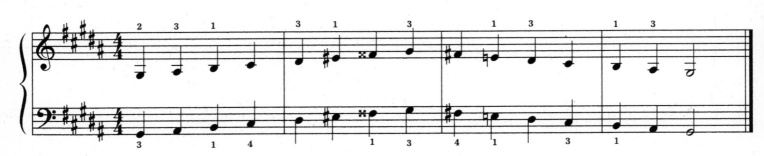

D# Natural Minor Scale

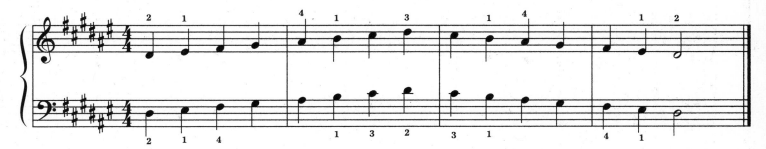

D# Harmonic Minor Scale

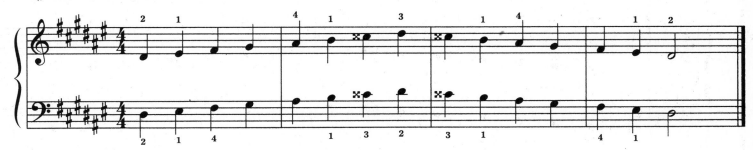

D# Melodic Minor Scale

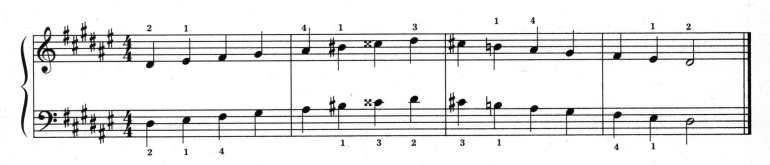

A# Natural Minor Scale

A# Harmonic Minor Scale

A# Melodic Minor Scale

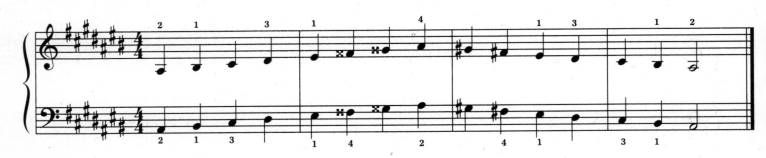

D Natural Minor Scale

D Harmonic Minor Scale

D Melodic Minor Scale

218

G Natural Minor Scale

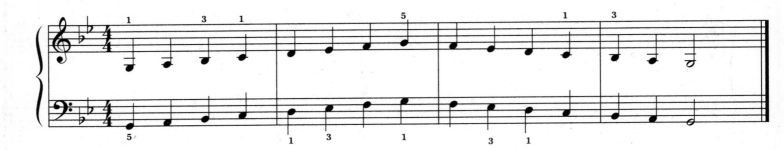

G Harmonic Minor Scale

G Melodic Minor Scale

C Natural Minor Scale

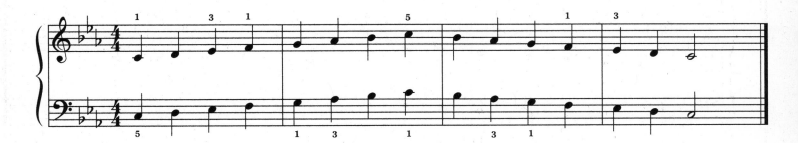

C Harmonic Minor Scale

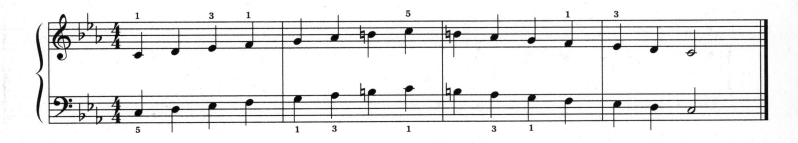

C Melodic Minor Scale

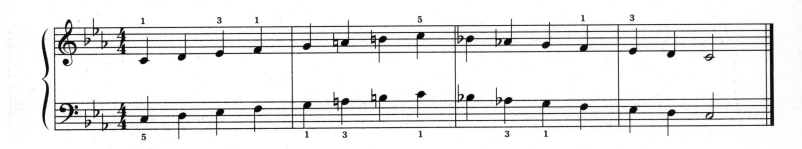

F Natural Minor Scale

F Harmonic Minor Scale

F Melodic Minor Scale

Bb Natural Minor Scale

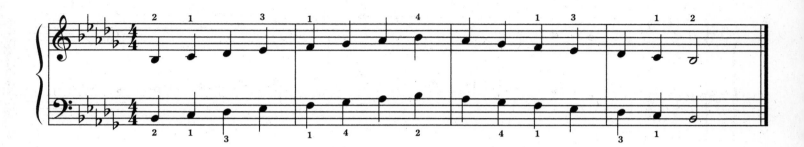

Bb Harmonic Minor Scale

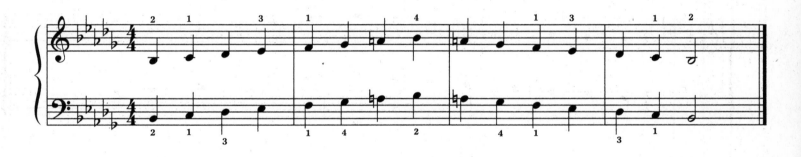

Bb Melodic Minor Scale

E♭ Natural Minor Scale

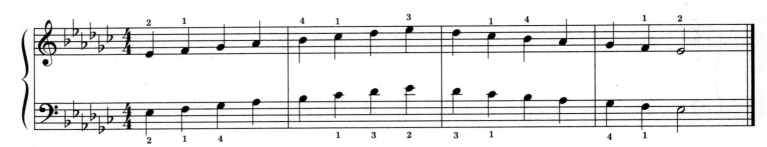

E♭ Harmonic Minor Scale

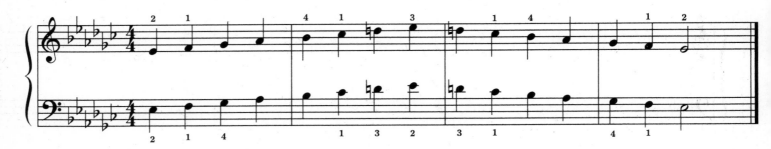

E♭ Melodic Minor Scale

A♭ Natural Minor Scale

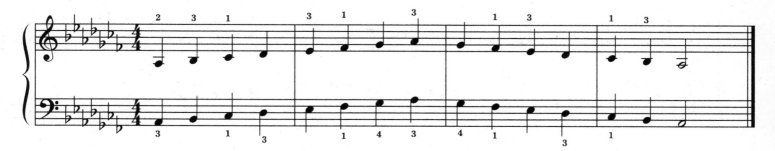

A♭ Harmonic Minor Scale

A♭ Melodic Minor Scale

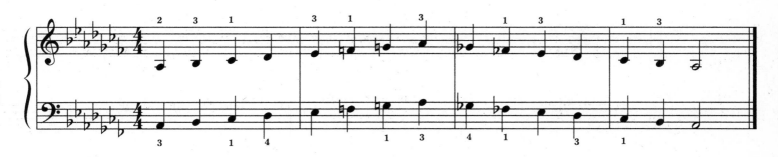

THE CIRCLE OF FIFTHS

The *circle of fifths* serves as a quick reference guide to the relationship of the keys and how key signatures can be figured out in a logical manner. Clockwise movement (up a 5th) provides all of the sharp keys by progressively adding one sharp to the key signature. Similarly, counter-clockwise (down a 5th) provides the flat keys by adding one flat.

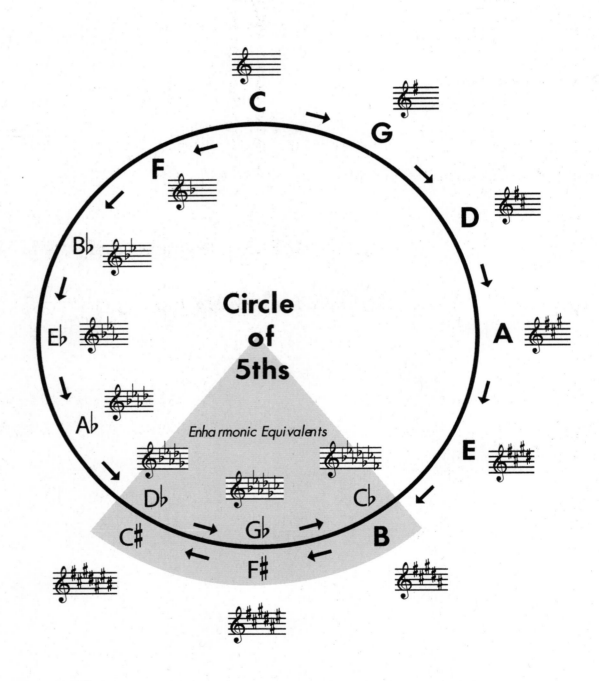

Circle of 5ths

Enharmonic Equivalents